F. Coming out and life beyond the closet

iv. Relationships

Roommates Can't Always Be Lovers

Lige Clarke and Jack Nichols

Roommates Can't Always Be Lovers

An Intimate Guide to Male-Male Relationships

ST. MARTIN'S PRESS   NEW YORK

To
Mary, Euphemia and Graham
and
Corinne, Shelbiana, Bramlette
and
George Cleon

ACKNOWLEDGMENTS

Many people have contributed to this book, particularly those who wrote to us with their puzzlements. If they hadn't done so, this book would never have seen daylight.

Members and friends of the Gay Liberation Front at the University of Colorado in Boulder were a great inspiration. They cared more for people than for theories. Glenda, Irene, Manny, Jonathan, Alan, Gregg, Christopher, and Darcy—we won't forget you!

Nor can we forget the friendships of those crusaders who sustained and influenced us through the 1960s: Dr. Franklin E. Kameny, theorist, the first person to fight the discriminatory policies of the U.S. Government; Kay Tobin, chronicler, author of *The Gay Crusaders* (Paperback Library); Barbara Gittings, scholar, Coordinator of the Task Force on Gay Liberation, American Library Association (Social Responsibilities Round Table); Foster Gunnison, Jr., farsighted archivist; Richard Inman, Florida's first crusader; Lilli Vincenz, a spokeswoman superb; Perrin Shaffer, tireless activist; and Rosalyn Regelson, strategist, the first "Professor of Homosexuality."

In the early 1970s we were fired by the good humor, enthusiasm and dedication of such people as Rich Wandel, Morty Manford, Don Goodwin, Jim Owles, Michael Miller, John Gish, Jerry Purpura and Rocky, Donn Teal, Allen Roskoff,

Dick Leitsch, Bob Amsel, George Hislop and Ron Shearer.

The people who worked with us when we were Editors of GAY are too numerous to mention, although we want to thank them all. Among those we can't fail to mention are Jim Buckley and Al Goldstein as well as Stefani Lyon, whom we shall miss. Thanks too to the newspaper's photographer, Eric Stephan Jacobs, who took the photo of us on the cover of this book.

For contributing a fine introduction we are indebted to Dr. George Weinberg, author of *Society and the Healthy Homosexual* (St. Martin's Press and Doubleday-Anchor Books). For editorial assistance Leslie Pockell has once again served well.

Finally, thanks to dear friends for their love and encouragement: to Steve Yates and Nick Ludwig in whose Fire Island abode we put much of this manuscript together, and to Richard Peters, Hank Kaufman, Howard Thompson, and Juan Martinez, who brighten our lives because they exist.

INTRODUCTION

by Dr. George Weinberg

Author of *Society and the Healthy Homosexual*

"The gay community" is a term used by many recent writers. Commonly, it implies a district to which homosexuals have migrated from far and wide. Many grew up anonymously in small towns and now enjoy the luxury of not having to conceal their homosexuality. One hears phrases like "The gay community was incensed at . . . ," phrases which make it unmistakable that the word "community" is used in its geographical sense.

But the gay community, thought of this way, represents a very small fraction of homosexuals. The majority, well over ninety percent, are still living anonymously. They are sprinkled across the country with miraculous randomness. Homosexuals are to be found in every kind of family, neighborhood, city and state. They wear every kind of clothing, have every kind of physique, and hold every kind of job. In fact, if a statistical genius had undertaken to scatter the homosexuals in our society randomly across the population, he could hardly have done as well.

To all but relatively few homosexual men and women in the

United States, the gay community remains a faraway place. These people read of marches and picketlines and court cases brought by professed homosexuals, and think of some happy band of people essentially different from themselves. To many, it is remote in time also—a society envisioned as existing off in the future, in some era when decency and self-respect are usual for homosexuals. The gay community is to these people synonymous with the promised land.

To Jack Nichols and Lige Clarke, the gay community exists already, and has no boundaries. It is not a region like Greenwich Village or Fire Island. It is not made up of only professed homosexuals. The authors conceptualize a larger gay community, one that includes all homosexual men and women. It is a scattered, diverse community. Many of its members are unidentified by their own families as homosexual, and by their friends.

These members all sense that the community exists. They share rights, interests, special problems. And they feel their connectedness. The word "homosexual" in a newspaper arrests their attention. Their impulse toward secrecy, however, keeps many of the members estranged, feeling insecure, unable to find listeners or to ask questions pertaining to their homosexuality.

Jack and Lige have been fighting for gay rights for over ten years. They have counseled many hundreds of homosexuals in all walks of life. They have led marches, and even picketed the White House. They founded and became editors of a newspaper for the gay community which they envisioned. The newspaper was uncompromising in its dedication to the community of homosexuals spread across the country.

In its innocuous-looking envelope the newspaper *Gay* went far and wide. It had readers of every age, some of whom in big cities were already activists, others who hardly knew they were homosexual, and others who had long known but had never met a single other homosexual in their whole lives. The suppression of information concerning homosexual life has been so thorough that until recently there were few references to the subject outside of books on mental illness. The thought that a person could be homosexual and still deserving of the right to discuss his or her outlook, and to ask questions, was horrifying. Newspapers guarded against reviewing books on the subject, and would not take ads for such books. Even magazines which obviously catered to homosexuals among others were reluctant to give space to the franker gay publications. In this context, the newspaper was startling. The fact that it was being delivered to people in all walks of life was revolutionary. Not too many years earlier, the publication *One*, which was for homosexuals, had found it necessary to go to the courts for permission to be distributed.

The timing was right for this bold new publication. Jack and Lige rounded up writers, not all homosexual, who believed in the cause of gay rights. And when the paper appeared, with articles on very diverse subjects and by many different people, the communication went in both directions. A plethora of letters came back to the newspaper. Some were from very young men, some from those who had been married a short time, a few from grandfathers. Some were from people with sexual problems —impotence, and from people worried about venereal diseases. Many concerned small-town living, the handling of gossip, and the issue of whether to tell people of being homosexual. There were numerous letters discussing problems of relationships, how to act in different sexual situations, how and where to meet people. Most of the letters were from men, doubtless because the authors are men. Not all were friendly. But all were informative.

To Jack and Lige as the editors of *Gay* went the task of answering nearly all of these letters. Collected, the letters provide a marvelously various sample of life in the gay community at large. In these letters, people voice their hopes and complaints. Just how representative are the letters of the thinking of homosexuals generally? In one sense, the people were unusual—they were all the· sort who would write a letter to someone they did not know, and to find it worthwhile to tell that person intimate facts about their lives. This takes a certain brand of optimism, the belief that other human beings might be genuine and would care about the lives of strangers. And it also takes courage. For every letter that was received, there were perhaps a dozen that were contemplated by people, or actually written and never sent. This is the counterpart of the situation with the newspaper itself. For every copy bought, there were many glimpsed at on newspaper stands and passed by, because the person was afraid to reveal interest in homosexuality, even to a newspaper dealer whom he could avoid seeing ever again.

It might be said that the letter writers were people with more problems than homosexuals as a group. If so, the letters stand as evidence for the general good spirits of homosexuals. True, some are from patently demoralized people. But the very preoccupations of most of the writers suggest that they are not on any course of disaster, merely perplexed about some issue. And no wonder, because the condemnation of homosexuality has made it hard for homosexuals to clarify basics, to communicate on matters of wide interest to homosexuals.

We cannot know for sure how good a sample of the thinking in the gay community is provided by the letters, because we have nothing better to compare them against. There is no one, and no institution, to whom homosexuals have written with any regularity; no organization that provided the sense of acceptance and the motivation for gay people to wish to bare their souls. The gay press is the one exception. In short, letters such as those which came to the newspaper are the best sampling of the diverse thought among homosexuals.

Jack and Lige have answered these letters in many different tones. The atmosphere they create in their answers is often more significant than what they actually say. They have an ear for seriousness. But they undercut self-righteousness. At other times, by taking an issue more lightly than the questioner, they throw it into perspective. The reader will find the answer for himself, if he feels relaxed enough to look for it. Errors will not be fatal, the authors seem to be saying. But beware of postponing the time for your dreams. I like them especially when they are rebutting the criteria of physical beauty according to which all but one person in ten thousand is ugly. The art of life consists largely in the ability to see beauty, to remain open to beauty, for nature never tires of showing it to us in new forms.

This book was made possible by the growing sense of community among homosexuals. And it certainly is a contribution to that sense of community.

January 1974
New York City

The hallmark of egotistical love, even when it masquerades as altruistic love, is the negative answer to the question "Do I want my love to be happy more than I want him to be with me?" As soon as we find ourselves working at being indespensable, rigging up a pattern of vulnerability in our loved ones, we ought to know that our love has taken the socially sanctioned form of egotism.

> *Germaine Greer*
> *in* The Female Eunuch

"I COULDN'T STAND TO BE
CALLED QUEER!"

Dear Lige and Jack,

I'm writing you because I have a problem; a real hangup. I am 21, 6'2'', 180 pounds, and, of course, I dig the male animal. I'm a head. I'm fairly good-looking and chicks hang on to me. I've been seeing the same chick for about two years. This brings me to my problem: I'd like to tell her where my head is at, but I'm afraid I'd lose her and she's very good for my ego. Our heads are on the same level. I think I love her, but my mind is so fucked up that I'm no longer sure.

All I know is that at the sight of a good-looking cat my own age, I get a feeling in my stomach that won't quit till my pants start sticking to my leg.

I'd like to tell my parents but it would kill them. They even said as much once.

There are very few people who are not heads that I can rap to, and this causes a very empty feeling. There must be some other gay heads my age, somewhere. But where do I find them? I don't dig fems. They turn me off. If I could find someone I could talk to—I mean really groove with—maybe I could come out in the open. But I'm not sure. Please be the sages of my Nirvana.

1

I'm so tired of playing the game of secrecy. I know it isn't fair to my girl, because I don't want to get married at this time. Neither does she. But I sometimes think that this would be the best thing for me to do, although I realize it would be selfish of me. If only people didn't put gay people down so. Man it can really hurt!

I guess that you know how it feels to be called queer. I couldn't stand that. Mainly because I'm not gay. What I need is someone to talk to. I think that's what I really need to ease my head.

If you know anyone I can rap to—someone who can dig his head and mine—please advise.

By the way, if you think that this letter will help anyone else in the same spot, you may print it, but I have to have my name withheld. I don't think that I'm ready for exposure as yet.

> Your friend,
> Jack O.
> Jackson Heights, New York

Dear Jack,

So "chicks" hang on to you, eh? Such a suave description of human relations! Luckily you realize that secrecy games with a loved one are a drag, whether it's a parent, a "chick" or a woman.

If your parents would die if you told them, don't tell them . . . at least unless you've got a few years to spare to convince them that dying isn't the coolest response.

Nowadays there are so many gay heads it's hard to understand how you've missed them. Try the nearest university's gay liberation group. They have regular campus meetings.

Can't say as anyone has called us queer. Demented, perhaps,

or spaced, but not queer. Anyway, a faggot by any other name would smell as sweet.

Quite truthfully, you don't have to get all uptight about choosing between the sexes. Make it easier on yourself and linger in varied locales where either of the sexes can choose you. It seems wise to like people because they have sexy minds instead of sweating over their genders or the exact size and shape of their physical apparatus.

Fortunately you realize that marriage is not the solution to *any* problem. Don't despair. Now that you can relax, breathe, and discover you're ok, that you're in good health (as long as you take good care of your six-foot-two bod) you've got thousands of joys ahead and if anyone's head—female or male—is good for you, they'll hang not only *on* you but *with* you—as the street urchins say—"*for days*."

AFTERWORD

Dear Lige and Jack,

Thanks very much for answering my letter.

Many things have changed since I last wrote you (all for the better). I now have a beautiful job. I work for a radio station as a writer, a talent that I never knew I had before, and I'm really digging it.

Something has happened that's nearly blown my mind. There's another cat at work that does the same job as I do. He is also a head so we established quick rapport. While we were rapping the other day he asked me if I wanted to come over to his crib and groove with his woman—just the four of us (implying me with mine). Until he asked me, I'd never told anyone that I was gay. I took a deep breath and said that I don't really dig women (which was a small lie) and he said that it was all right

3

and that I should come anyway. The three of us had a really beautiful time. They're beautiful people and I had a chance to explain to them how I dug sex with girls and guys alike but that I dug guys more.

Later, the three of us ended in bed together (none of us is sure how it happened, but it did). It was then that I realized that I am not gay nor am I straight. I'm me and that's a good feeling. I don't know if it's possible to clear your head in just one night, but I think that is just what I did. I'm planning to tell my girl about my thing tonight and if she doesn't dig it then we are not as right for each other as I thought. Either way, I'm not going to let anything stand in my way anymore. I finally am in a state where I like myself and that can't be bad (as long as I don't start to like myself too much—but I don't think there is a danger of that).

I think the world is on the verge of a sexual awakening, and I want to help. I now feel very clean and I want to help clean up the dirt that's been smeared on the gay world and the straight one too, for that matter.

Fondest regards,
Jack O.
Jackson Heights, New York

•

"I'VE NEVER HAD SEX"

Dear Lige and Jack,
I have an immense problem: I don't know where I belong in society. I haven't had sex with either men or women even though I've always wanted to.

I have always gotten satisfaction out of reading books about men or looking at pictures of them. More satisfaction, I think, than I get from reading about or looking at pictures of women.

But please don't get me wrong. I don't read books and look at pictures of men solely for getting a hardon or for masturbating. I can't give you any reason why I prefer men to women. What I wish to ask you is this: what am I to do to find my sanity and my place in society? I am very lonely and it's cold out here.

Since I have not discussed my problem with anybody else, I would respectfully adhere to whatever you recommend (to a certain point). The reason is that I am extremely afraid of reprisals from people who don't think or believe in what I think I believe in.

Enclosed is one of the very few photos ever taken of me to help you make some sort of decision, even if it is just to tell me to get lost!

> Respectfully yours,
> Charles W.
> Fort Wayne, Indiana

Dear Charles,

If you are "extremely afraid" of reprisals from people who don't "think or believe" the same as you do, your ball game is lost before it starts.

It sounds as though you expect rejection. Maybe that's why you haven't had sex with either men or women. A picture book filled with handsome men isn't nearly as much fun as the real thing.

The first thing for you to do is go to meetings of your local gay lib group in Ft. Wayne. Make some friends. Don't be afraid. Nobody is going to gobble you up. And if you don't meet anybody you're comfortable with, go to Chicago—ask the gay liberation group there about interesting places to go.

If you feel at home in the gay world—swell. There's plenty of room for every kind of person—for those who return to the opposite sex too—just as long as such persons don't go off in a corner forever and refuse to be civil to old friends. So you need never worry about developing relationships with women if you feel so inclined. If you like men better, don't worry about it. The things we really and truly enjoy are usually good for us. It's the things we feel lukewarm about that are not usually as necessary as we think.

But do get out and explore! Live a little. You have nothing to lose but your virginity.

• • •

COMING OUT   PART I

Coming out, gay slang for discovering one's homosexual capacities, is something that happens to men and women no matter what their age, social class, religion, or ethnic origin.

Sometimes it is a difficult and lonely process. As the discovery begins such people may assume that they're "the only ones" in the world. Today, luckily, this painful notion is fading, thanks to widened public knowledge. Nevertheless, more than a few who are coming out carry weighty cargoes of misconceptions, apprehensions, and hesitancies into their experience. There are letters in this book which demonstrate that this is so.

Once a decision to come out has been made, those who've made the decision usually experience an overwhelming sense of relief. They begin to appreciate some of the truly comforting characteristics of the gay subculture. Among younger people this relief sometimes takes

6

the form of telling everybody, family and non-gay friends. Some are angry at society, for a while at least. Having been taught to fear their gay comrades and finding that such fear is based on ignorance, they're annoyed because they've been duped. As they mature, however, such annoyance mellows into a better understanding of what has taken place.

Most people who come out, however, don't make a big fuss. They keep their love lives private and are likely to punch time clocks on weekday mornings after struggling to get to work with the rest of the masses.

A difficulty with coming out is that it frequently becomes a dead-end experience rather than a continual process. Coming out too often stops abruptly with the discovery of social institutions like gay bars and clubs, the acquiring of a few new friends, and going to parties or dances. The individual who has come out learns that joining the company of the homosexually inclined masses is not nearly as fearful a transgression as he'd once been indoctrinated to think.

He decides that while gay society may not be the best of all possible worlds, it's as good as any other, and he settles into a somewhat lethargic self-acceptance bordering on apathy. Gay people have no deeper knowledge of their sexuality or its implications than anybody else does. Aside from what seems to be the occasional need to hide one's feelings from a boss, a neighbor, or a maiden aunt or, perhaps, to swap gay jokes at the local pub, most people who think of themselves as gay are far more concerned with the same everyday diversions that occupy their fellow "straights."

Some, who find it discomfiting to think about being different, may make deliberate attempts to ignore homosexuality as a topic. But lurking underneath their mild manners one can frequently sense guilts, fears, hostilities and a host of old-fashioned myths.

Socrates said that the unexamined life is not worth living. While we would not be nearly so harsh, it does seem possible that an unexamined life presents roadblocks to happiness. A man who has failed to fully accept his sexuality, for example, and who cannot revel in its beauty, may be willing to receive watered-down affection from others without realizing that he's being cheated. If only he had thought to come out in a fuller sense, instead of stumbling about in the dark corners of curious subterfuges, he would have discovered capabilities far beyond his present ones. Suppose he has settled for a regular routine of one-night stands because involving himself too openly with someone of his own sex he feels is going too far. Into his home comes a parade of bodies but he remains without interest in people as individuals. Genuine friendliness and an exchanged appreciation of intriguing ingredients of character are missing from his life.

In the rush of urban chaos, quickie sex (the sort which divides one's larger life from one's sex life) often seems to suffice for months at a time, particularly for those who are on tight weekly work schedules. What starts early in one's experience as a way of avoiding involvement can become a lifestyle that leaves in its wake a genuine emptiness. People who chop their lives into well-screened compartments under the illusion that they are "out" may never have a chance to look back on their gay experiences as some of the warmest, wisest, wittiest and most loving moments they could possibly imagine. This happens as long as their concept of coming out has reached a dead end and hampers their discovery of intimacy. Not only do they miss the chance to explore more fully their own

8

emotional/sexual life, but they fail to see how such discoveries expand their creative energies.

Comradeship, even if it does not include sexual proximity, is one of the great advantages offered by gay society. Since what is called "the gay world" is less formal than the socially structured world-at-large, sexual relationships that don't turn into love affairs can still become good friendships. Often we see young men who've recently come out trailing in the company of people who are scarcely like them in either disposition or posture. These fellows may think they've come out and that the gay friends they've made are typical of all men similarly inclined. And because they don't realize that gay society is as heterogeneous as it is they remain in tightly knit circles —failing to explore the wider world beyond. Sometimes, after giving "gay life" a whirl, these poor blokes return to their closets.

Coming out should include more than an enthusiasm for the innate goodness of one's own sensibilities. It should encompass knowledge of the varieties of the gay subculture. Irrational fears must disappear along with reverence for whatever the "fashionable" guardians of the status quo may be insisting upon this week.

Coming out means exploring and absorbing new vistas in the self. It means discovering the body, for example, and learning through our own experience about *touch*, putting behind us the old groping, clutching and grasping of the past, the sort that showed how uncertain we were that our sexuality was good because it was also (in those days) retiring and sometimes furtive. In this age of growing leisure, we will all be faced with long hours to explore ourselves and others, and *coming out* should include a self-taught awareness of such processes.

9

AN ADVENTUROUS MARINE

Dear Lige and Jack,
I am writing this letter concerning one of your articles I read last night. The article I am talking about was about Fire Island and next to the article there was a big photo of one of you guys and you were nude. I admired this picture very much and couldn't help but think of how nice it would be just to be in bed with you. The way you talked about this place called Fire Island made me wish I was there today.

Right now I am in the United States Marines and have been for eleven months. They are giving me a medical discharge next week for having homosexual tendencies. I will be a civilian again and my only wish is to do a lot of traveling and finding new adventure. If there is any way in the world I could ever get to meet you please let me know. I am 19 years old and have dirty-blond hair. I am 5'9'' and weigh 150 pounds, medium complexion. You, I already know what you look like from the photo. Very cute indeed.

> Love
> Fred S.
> North Carolina

Dear Fred,
Everything you said thrilled us. There's only one problem, a small one perhaps, but a problem nevertheless. The picture you saw was not one of us. It was of a paid model, and unfortunately, we don't even know the guy or we'd send your letter to him so he could have the option of putting himself on your travel itinerary.

Have fun traveling. We hope you meet lots of men who are as beautifully straightforward as you—as direct and as honest.

"ITS HARD TO FIND A LOVER"

Dear Lige and Jack,

I'm writing you for some honest advice. Why is it so hard to find a lover? It seems that making a million dollars or going to the moon is easier. But finding an individual to love, have fun with and identify with is almost impossible. I've been looking for a lover for quite some time now. I go to bars, baths, the Firehouse, take long walks, go to the park and you name it. I go with the intention of finding that guy that I can settle down with—make a home with. I'm twenty-five, quite good-looking, have a good, solid job that pays well, a beautiful apartment, a good family life; I'm very discreet with whom I have sex, maybe once a month or so, and I'm very sincere with whomever I meet. I'm not demanding or difficult to get along with and have no significant hang-ups, except finding a lover. My friends say that I really have everything, looks, money, a head on my shoulders, but they don't believe me when I say I would be happier poor and broke living in a run-down apartment with a guy that I'm happy with.

So what advice am I asking for? What am I doing wrong? Where can I go, who can I talk to, what should I do? I'm looking for a small, young guy who wants to have an older hunky lover. I'm well built, around six feet tall and enjoy sex with younger, smaller guys. I'm sincere, tired of running around and would like to sit around some evenings and watch good old TV for a change.

Thanks and will be waiting for your answer.

Love,
Mike A.
New York City

11

Dear Mike,

Luckily you realize that you do have one hang-up, at least, and that is your intense desire to find a lover and the fact that you spend most of your free time with this one goal in mind. While it is a perfectly fine intention, it comes about naturally and with ease if you don't try too hard. Like floating in water: if you try too hard, you sink. Jesus said that those who try to save their souls shall lose them. Get the point? Anyway, we'd say this: learn to enjoy your own company and yourself first. Strive to be independent, to look independent, to be well-centered in both body and mind. Men are attracted to men who are self-assured. Often, if a person is seeking outside of himself for happiness, others can sense it and are not interested. Stay shy of jealous types (who are insecure) and strike up more than one friendship at a time. A stronger relationship should develop naturally with one of your many friends—the one you get along with best. But don't look for a somebody to sit under the apple tree only with you. If love is as wonderful as you believe it to be, it belongs to everybody. Reach out and touch everyone with loving kindness, enjoy the radiance and strength of your own outgoing feelings, and other men will gravitate toward you like (as Marlene sings) "moths around a flame."

One last word about hang-ups. Don't look for one "type" so specifically. A preference for only a "small, young guy" is a severe hang-up that keeps you from enjoying a larger selection of people. Don't think badly of "one-night stands" either. A relationship has to start somewhere, and one night is as good as any other, only not in front of a TV set. TV spells the death of any good relationship!

• • •

MEETING SOMEONE

How does one cope with *rejection*? How can it be avoided? How does one increase one's batting average? What are the secrets of attracting a beautiful person?

When a person experiences the humiliation of seeing his natural warmth and friendliness rejected snootily by a seeming Adonis, he must realize that the problem lies not in himself but in the "Adonis." A beautifully proportioned young man who has not learned to emit loving (though not necessarily sexual) vibrations when he is appreciated is to be pitied. Usually he's cold, inept and insecure. More often than not, he's really unattractive to a truly perceptive person, one who looks for character and warmth. Would it injure Adonis to crack his cool with a friendly smile, even if he doesn't follow it with conversation? Hardly. Only a man who feels no reservoir of beauty *within* considers a compliment an assault on his privacy.

The person who offers such a compliment must be sure, in fact, that that is what he *is* offering. It makes a difference as to how one's friendliness is proffered. If it is a hard-core leer, a stony sex-plea (instead of warmth and friendliness), a handsome man may have a perfect right to turn away. He wishes, after all, to be appreciated for qualities he has which go deeper than those which are obvious. He knows he's handsome. A sexually motivated stare tells him nothing except that someone else knows it too. He's used to it. But a warm and friendly grin lets him know that its bearer may possibly think that he too is warm and friendly and thus he feels complimented. It makes a difference.

Too often extremely attractive men fail to receive the kind of subtle appreciation they crave. When they're approached on a sexual level *only*, they flee. Those who do

13

approach them on this level are guilty of reinforcing their seemingly cold exteriors. If our relationships with beautiful men are to be democratized, then those who would draw close to them must begin to look for what they themselves consider their most intriguing characteristic: an inner beauty.

There's no foolproof way to guarantee success in the initiation of new relationships. There are, however, prime tips which do serve the cause of improved communication. Whether a man can successfully follow such tips will depend to a great extent on his *sense of self*—because it is on this, more than on anything else, that real magnetism depends.

Self-confidence and self-assurance are bared automatically in one's expression, in one's movements and in the way one holds oneself. A person who is not secure *within* is easily spotted—his eyes dart hopefully from one prospect in a room to the next. He finds himself unable to stay in one spot and wanders about surveying faces, hoping for a response.

The single most attractive attribute a man can show is a calm self-content, a characteristic that certifies he's anchored to a "center" within and that he's not anxiously pursuing assurance from others. Clothing, jewelry, hairstyle, or bright and witty topics of conversation are easily seen through. But a man aware of his own worth is genuine. Perhaps Walt Whitman was talking of such men when he said:

I and mine do not convince by arguments,
Similes, rhymes,
We convince by our presence.

14

One of the prime obstacles to meaningful encounters lies in the mind of the person who hopes for one. It involves his demand for a "type." Just how specific this sort of demand can become is apparent in the "personals" columns of gay tabloids, where ads are placed asking for "get-togethers" for "good times." "Must be blond, under 24, tall," or "prefer hairy, dark-skinned, stocky builds," or "youthful appearance a MUST," or "no one under 30 need apply." To say that such "seekers after love" are *preference-prone* is an understatement. Exceedingly shallow requirements have created a need for them to specify *in print* the "types" that they're failing to meet in the course of everyday living. Just how widespread is this inflexible selectivity? One need only listen to the conversations of gesticulating bar patrons to overhear such comments as, "Oh, he's very nice and very handsome but he's not my type."

Preferences are an inalienable right but they may be carried to extremes. When this happens, a man needlessly eliminates his own chances to be sociable. He puts a muzzle on himself and then complains because he has no lover.

Another attractive trait, one that seldom fails to draw favorable attention, is *affirmation*. Almost everyone likes a man who says "yes" to life, who is optimistic and happy. Most people are out on the town for a good time. They don't like to be brought down by clever cynicism or strident pessimism. A person whose mind dwells on the unfortunate things of life is not thought to be a lucky charm.

A happy demeanor can't really be faked, of course. It shows in the eyes and in the set of the jaw. It is particularly obvious in a man's posture. To acquire this trait means that a certain kind of spiritual revolution must take place *within*, and this can be brought about, usually, by conscious self-care, which leads, in turn, not only to vitality and good health, but to a carefree self-esteem.

Those who have a difficult time meeting the men of their dreams are also poor listeners. They assume that they must *impress*, and they often compose a mental checklist of topics which they themselves think are impressive. The approach usually has the reverse affect since the determination to impress is so easily detected. Younger people, particularly, and those with little or no social experience, are sometimes given to such jittery stridence. It can take serious forms bordering on pompousness. At other times it spills out as a Pandora's box of humorous annecdotes, usually told at such high speed that the gentlemen, who it is hoped will be impressed, can't tell where one story ends and another begins. Most everyone enjoys being appreciated and a person who insists on stage center at every opportunity indicates that he wants *all* attention. He's failed to notice his new companion's more intriguing peculiarities. Too bad. He loses.

The secret of attracting beautiful men lies in one's ability to *feel*, because of inner attitudes, that one is beautiful too. Socially prescribed "good looks" don't count nearly as much as many assume they do. Homely men can be extremely attractive and "good-looking" men can be quite ugly. There's a pronounced difference between being homely and ugly, and it becomes clear in *attitude*. A healthy attitude reflects itself in the body and is the lodestar of cronies, playmates and chums. What most men need to discover is their own inner strength and beauty, utilizing such knowledge quietly in their demeanor. When they have begun, as a result, to take their own attractiveness for granted it then becomes easy to find links and affinities with other beautiful people on an equal footing.

16

TEA TOTALLER

Dear Lige and Jack,
It seems like everywhere I go these days, to parties, dinners and even on dates, someone is always insisting that I smoke a joint. So what if everyone else is doing it, does that mean I should be pushed into doing it also? Sometimes when I refuse, people treat me as though I'm an outcast.

I don't want anything to do with drugs though I will drink a little from time to time. How could I best handle this situation?

Kenneth P.
Boston, Massachusetts

Dear Kenneth,
Grow long hair and a moustache and tell new friends you've smoked for years but that it all bores you now. Don't seem shy. It's your naiveté and an unwillingness to experiment that your friends object to, and if you succeed in making them feel that grass is "old hat" to you, or that you are into "meditation," "yoga," or other disciplines that expand consciousness without psychedelics, you can turn the tables and make them feel old-fashioned when they insist that the inhalation of smoke is superior to your esoteric system of self-enlightenment.

If this doesn't work, say it makes you wet the bed.

•

STRAIGHT A HET

Dear Lige and Jack,
I wish you would stop using the word "straight" as the opposite of Gay. Straight means right, correct, usual, ordinary, normal,

truth, fairness, honesty, accurate, upright, reliable, candid. Its antonymns are tricky, dishonest, crooked, swindler, abnormal, devious, dissolute, unnatural and vicious (per *Funk & Wagnall's Dictionary*.) When straight is used to mean heterosexual, you imply that Gay is abnormal, unnatural, etc.

The continued use of straight has an undesirable subconscious psychological effect on the readers and militates against pride, self-esteem and causes Gays to think of themselves in a negative manner.

The non-prejudicial word "Het" is now being used as the antonym of Gay. Why don't you adopt the new usage?

> Peace, sex, joy
> Don J.
> Los Angeles, California

Dear Don,
Your point is well-taken, although the word "Het" sounds rather like some minor Egyptian deity. In 1951, D. W. Cory made note of your criticism in *The Homosexual in America*. Now, in this age of "sexism" there are innumerable word squabbles and so we've allowed newspaper columnists the words they prefer.

"Straight" in New York's East Village parlance means "linear," that is to say, "logic oriented, mechanistic, and conventionally rational." A straight person is one who is tied to the "straight and narrow." In this sense the word "straight" is negative but does not necessarily refer to heterosexuals. There are some very "straight" homosexuals running around.

●

BASIC VOCABULARY?

Dear Lige and Jack,
Please tell me what the following terms mean:
1. fellatio
2. Greek
3. French
4. hard-core
5. fornication

Gay Power!
Thanks,
Phil
Buffalo, New York

Dear Phil,
You're amazing! We never thought we'd hear from someone willing to sign off with "Gay Power!" before knowing what fellatio meant.

The Queen's Vernacular, A Gay Lexicon by Bruce Rodgers (Straight Arrow Press), defines "fellatio" rather bluntly as "sucking cock."

The word "Greek" refers to a lovely pastime that was common in the cradle of Western civilization: namely, anal intercourse.

"French" connotes the practice of any form of oral copulation. Kissing, licking, cocksucking, muff-diving and the like are all lackluster words describing "Frenching"—a much maligned delight that's always in need of good words spoken on its behalf.

"Hard-core" is an adjective used to indicate explicit sexual acts—usually with the male organ fully erect—depicted in books, pictures and films.

"Fornication" is one of those illicit-sounding words that is now taking on humorously acceptable connotations. Any sexual act which does not take place between a man and his wife is fornication. Premarital sex is fornication. Same-sex relations are fornication. Many Bible-thumpers fail to appreciate that fornication is needed today.

•

A ROSE BY ANY OTHER NAME

Dear Lige and Jack,

I very much dislike the word "gay." I avoid using it whenever possible. I'm much prouder to be a homosexual. Gay is still a euphemism for "fairy" to me. I'm speaking only of male homosexuals, of course. Essentially it describes the shallow, superficial, fastidious, effeminate homosexual. Everybody dislikes shallowness and superficiality; sweet sensitivity in a male is very beautiful but effeminacy is seldom so. "Gay" is strongly allied with camp, the game of a fool who's rejected himself as a real human being. It reaches the height of unpleasantness for me in the mouths of those who lovingly roll its pronunciation to "gaaaaaeeeee"—giving it the feel of silk underwear.

Presuming that it does describe the individual whom society has disdainfully labeled a fairy, who is beautiful with a beauty that society has refused to see, it may seem ugly because society has taught me to find it so. Maybe I'm a hapless victim of a male chauvinist society who may one day open his eyes and spiritually embrace the expression "gay." At the present time, however, it doesn't describe the intelligent, sensitive, strong, vi-

20

brant, vital homosexual being whom I find supremely beautiful. I gag at the thought of Leonardo's being "gay."

> Sincerely,
> Harvey B.
> Sacramento, California

Dear Harvey,
Leonardo wasn't GAY. He was QUEER!

•

GAY GAY GAY

Dear Piscean Spirits,
I really don't like the word "gay." Why should homosexuals be any more gay or happy than heteros—or sad for that matter. If hippies can change to yippies or flower people, why can't we?
Your Scorpio brother.

> Gene K.
> New Orleans, Louisiana

Dear Gene,
Why confine the word "gay" to homosexually inclined people? We prefer not to use it as a noun, but as an adjective. To us, the word indicates a life-style or an attitude. Haven't you ever known any gay "straights"? Some of our best friends are gay "straights."

•

CAN'T ALWAYS GET IT ON

Dear Lige and Jack,

I've been out only a short time and I have a problem. You see I can't always get it up for somebody. One or two guys who have been around for a while have told me that if you can't get it up all the time something's wrong with you. I'm puzzled and somewhat frustrated since I'd like to meet more people on a more personal level than strictly sex. I'm afraid this might have an effect on what they think of me as a person. It's important for me to make friends since I have decided that gay is good and I feel better now that I don't hide it. Yet due to these experiences I feel like some kind of cheap whore. Is it peculiar not to always be able to get a hard-on? Is there something wrong with me?

Tim J.
Tallahassee, Florida

Dear Tim,

There's nothing wrong with you simply because there are times you can't get it up. Many things influence our abilities, such as how tired we are at the time, how much we really feel attracted to someone, how relaxed our partner is, how much we've been drinking, eating, etc. Those supposedly experienced guys are all wet. Don't let anybody else's opinion upset you. The person who is put off by the fact that you don't perform on a particular occasion is only looking at your plumbing anyway and not at the really important you. A man capable of friendship won't be upset by an occasional night off. If this happens often, though, unrelated to physical problems, it may indicate a slight problem. A person new to sexual experience may still feel nervous and this can affect him in bed. If that's the case, the trick is to

22

turn your intellect off, put your mind to sleep and learn to pursue sexual pleasures uninhibitedly.

•

17-YEAR ITCH

Dear Lige and Jack,
We've been together for seventeen years and are both in our late thirties. Our sexual relationship has narrowed to the point of almost being nil, maybe twice a month. I find that I desire more sexual contact than he does. I'm basically not a promiscuous person and hate to have to go outside my own home for sex. Although my lover is healthy and strong he doesn't seem as interested. What's the best way to get him to take notice of me again?

> Sincerely,
> Charles S.
> Denver, Colorado

Dear Charles,
First, don't bug him with incessant questions about why he's not interested in you. Turn your attention to yourself while, at the same time, you perform special acts around the house to let him know you still love him and care for him. A special meal. New decorations. A present or two.

Spend more time—privately—grooming your own physique. It's a good sort of meditation. Take walks on your own to cultural spots: to parks, to city gardens, and regain that sexy sense of self that comes—some days—when you're striding along the street and can feel "the talk of those turning eyeballs." When you yourself are once again feeling

23

attractive—even to yourself—he'll feel your magnetism.

Perhaps you're spending too much time in a single bedroom. Lovers weren't meant to make love day after day, month after month and year after year in one changeless locale. Go away to a motel, or to a cabin in the woods. Visit friends in another city or lie together on some deserted beach.

Break old habit patterns. It is all too easy to slip into them and it is better to move from one residence to another or even from one city to another than to risk stagnation by sitting in the same chairs day and night.

Are you helping him find and expand his real interests? In any case, twice a month after seventeen years ain't so bad. Nothing to panic about, be sure.

•

THE BATHS

Dear Ones,

I would rather doubt that the Baths are anything but what they are—an outlet for the egoism, repression and oppression of one's sexual hang-ups.

As you yourself said, "If you're really a healthy, together person, you won't need to play games." Aren't the Baths merely a manifestation of real life? For if all people were healthy, together persons, there would be no need for gay baths, straight or gay bars, trucks, role playing, exploitation, etc. All people can't relate to each other as complete, open honest sexual human beings, and express physically their enjoyment of each other. I live in hope it may "come together."

> Peace,
> Jim S.
> Seattle, Washington

Dear Jim,

While what you say is perfectly true, it's also true that someone might use Baths or other such places to discover more about people and about himself. The danger of spending too much time in any type location is that one can too often make the mistake of assuming that it's the whole world.

Human behavior in both bars and Baths labors under a ton of etiquette. Etiquette, says Lao Tzu, stifles our natural sympathies.

● ● ●

NEW STYLES IN CRUISING

Cruising, gay slang for finding a chum, is generally adapted to an individual's personality. There's no set pattern or method and even the experiences of a man who's cruised for decades can't be relied on as sage. Fashions change from one decade to the next and behavior patterns set in the Fearful Fifties look peculiar to the straightforward young man of today. In the past men often followed one another for blocks, looking into store windows, stopping on street corners and eyeing each other, unable to say hello.

Today's successful cruisers are more likely to smile and to greet one another in a direct way. In the past, there was a tendency for men to inquire of one another what they might be likely to "do" in bed. This practice luckily has become quaint, at least among those who consider themselves well rounded. Patterns of dominance and passivity, borrowed in days of yore from conventional society, are also vanishing. Today's young men pride themselves on being versatile, knowing that it is just as blessed to receive as it is to give.

25

CRUISING IN A CLOSET

Dear Jack and Lige,

I really have a problem and I've just got up enough nerve to write to you. Perhaps you can help. But please do not divulge my name to anyone for the following reasons:

I am a married man, fifty years of age, white, have married children and am a grandfather. Two years ago I had a prostate operation and since then I have been losing my potency to such an extent that I can no longer hold an erection long enough to have complete intercourse. It seems to get limp in the process.

As a result, I am getting a feeling that I would like to perform fellatio on a clean, wholesome man, over twenty-one years of age. I cannot approach anyone even though I would like to. I'm a respected citizen in my community. If my wife should ever become aware of this letter, I am sure I would be in great trouble. But what I do without her knowledge is my business. So you see why I cannot afford to have her know what my feelings are. I am certain you understand.

As I have never done this before—that is, to perform fellatio—I don't know whether the feeling of a hard penis during fellatio would give me the sexual satisfaction I am looking for but in the absence of my own erection it is possible that I could and would enjoy someone else's.

I am sure you are not lacking in aquaintances who would submit to a novice and I would greatly appreciate your sending me the names of your friends with whom I could make contact. For obvious reasons I cannot furnish you with my telephone number, but I am enclosing a self-addressed, stamped envelope for your reply.

A sincere individual,
Philadelphia, Pennsylvania

Dear Sincere Individual:

We think you are fooling yourself when you rationalize cock-sucking as you do. To touch another person you need no heavy explanation—even if that other person is of the same sex. But must you limit your touch only to the hard—what is the proper word?—penis? Men have other anatomical features, too, you know. Eyes to stare into. Souls to explore.

Before you go sneaking around with men, luv, why not apply your eager mouth to your wife's little lovepot? Chances are it would improve your homelife immensely.

For obvious reasons, since you cannot furnish your telephone number, we cannot furnish you with the name of any self-respecting homosexually inclined gentleman.

If all you're interested in is a hard cock, try going to one of the local gay baths. But if you're interested in relationships of a wider nature, drop in on your local gay lib group. Or even, perhaps, your local gay church! Judging by your letter you seem to be the churchgoing type.

•

SWEET 15!

Dear Lige and Jack,

I don't know where to begin. It took me about a month to get up enough courage to go into the Oscar Wilde Book Store to get some literature on being gay. I'd go down to the Village and walk past the store a dozen times, only to return home without going in after spending a fortune on the subway. I finally got up the guts to go in. When I left, I felt something I'd never felt before. Call it fulfillment, relief, happiness, I don't know. Just being there and knowing that there were other people like me and knowing that I wasn't alone made me feel fantastic.

Now I'd really like to get involved in the movement, and meet people and everything but I run into one colossal problem: I'm fifteen and my parents don't know I'm gay, so that rules out meetings and social activities which are usually at night. If I told my father about myself, I'd probably get thrown out of the house or else never trusted again. I've never had any experience and I'm getting frustrated before I even start. Help! What can I do?

Love ya,
Robbi
Brooklyn, New York

Dear Robbi,
There's still plenty of time to explore and discover the whole terrain. Take advantage of your family's love—as long as they're not actually evil—and enjoy their roof under which you may delight in your growing knowledge of yourself for the next few years.

Don't make any big thing out of being gay. It's just an attraction to your own sex, that's all. So you're glad to know you're not the only one on the block? There are millions who probably share your racier fantasies.

Since you're close to Manhattan, you'll probably make many daytime friends. Choose your friends because they are fun to be with and because they're honest but not because they share certain sexual preferences. A sexual preference tells us very little about who is and who isn't a good friend. A warm smile is more important.

●

ONE WORKS AS WELL AS TWO

Dear Lige and Jack,
I recently contracted an infection and had to have one of my
testes removed. I'm twenty years old so I should have a lot of
life left in me, or I did before this happened.

I have a lover and he tells me that it doesn't make any
difference to him but I know that my performance in bed is
nothing like it used to be. Is there anything I can do to regain my
lost power?

> Yours truly,
> Arthur F.
> Bronx, New York

Dear Arthur,
There's nothing physical about your "lost power." The only
reason men have two testes in the first place is for insurance
against the loss of one of them. One teste works just as well as
two; the problem is all in your head. When your lover tells you it
doesn't matter you should listen to him. He's right. Actually
most sexual problems seem to arise out of fear and misunder-
standing and are not the products of physical causes. Just relax a
bit and you'll quickly find, we hope, that your powers will
renew themselves.

•

IT'S WHAT YA DO WITH
WHAT YA GOT

Dear Lige and Jack,
Is there any way to increase the size of the penis? I know the

29

answer is invariably "no," yet I am asking you once again. My penis measures a bare six inches in fullest erection. Soft, it is about three and a half inches and is especially embarrassing when I wear tight pants. I am forty-six and this matter of organ size continues to torment me as it did at twenty. All my experience has confirmed my belief that everyone (heterosexual and homosexual) considers organ size before any other attribute in a prospective sex partner. This "dirty old man" is still hoping there may be some way to do something about his limitation or learn to live comfortably with it.

Sincerely yours,
Walter W.
Phoenix, Arizona

Dear Walter,
There is no known method of increasing the size of the penis, so you must forget this fantasy once and for all. You can wear tight jeans if you like, but there's no need to display your genitals. That tactic is for hustlers, not self-respecting men; it's also a gambit for those who believe they have nothing else to offer anyone. Is this what you think about yourself? Forty-six is far from old. You have a great deal more to offer than a penis. If that is all your sex partners want, they don't want you, only a utensil.

Your belief that everyone considers organ size *first* is totally erroneous. Only those popeyed folk known as "size queens" do that. Most people (despite your belief) look for a great deal more than size, such as personality, interesting appearance and fields of mutual interest: all those things that make real live human beings.

Nobody should spend his life worrying about size. How uninhibited are you? Movement excites men—and touching.

30

Explore your senses slowly. Enjoy yourself and stop torturing yourself needlessly.

•

SEMEN SWALLOWING

Dear Lige and Jack,
I am a steady reader of yours. I have a question that seems ridiculous; I don't know if you can answer it, but maybe you can tell me who can.

I'm a female and a great lover of oral sex. I indulge in sex extravagantly.

Last week a friend of mine told me that male semen contains male hormones and can be harmful to me.

Recently at a group scene I was made by a woman and found it quite enjoyable. I have done this a few times since. My friend said it could have been the male hormones that made me enjoy another woman.

Is this true? What can they do to me?

Sincerely,
C. W.
Westbury, New York

Dear C.W.,
If you're enjoying the company of women you should, by your friend's logic, be able to swallow female juices which will give you female hormones, reverse your desires and return you to men. It is curious too that your friend's theory doesn't explain why gay men don't switch to women in droves.

Swallowing semen, be it a man's or a woman's, has never had much of an effect on anybody. Benefits may include a taste of

31

protein, maybe, but you'd do better to boil a couple of eggs for that.

● ● ●

MYTH MANUFACTURERS IN OUR MIDST

In a social milieu as confusing as the gay subculture often is to newcomers, the inept and the guilt-ridden have an easy time spreading their nonsense. There are those who insist that one is washed up after thirty. Others announce—unhesitatingly—that gay people are never punctual. A common theme they broadcast is that the homosexually inclined are not capable of longlasting relationships.

It's amazing how many pristine mentalities run loose in gay society, men who are the inheritors of sexual perspectives devised by Mrs. Grundy. One would think that a gay person's contact with a social substratum so uninhibitedly free (in contrast to the "freedom" that the more conventional masses enjoy) would make him carefree and shameless. But no. There are always those in gay circles, as in the world at large, who carry old-fashioned sexual recipes with them into their beds—and folks who get close to them must sleep on the crumbs.

How can we spot such dolts? It's easy. They have negative viewpoints. The people they know, and the problems they've encountered have been unfortunate.

Often, their contacts have been limited to barflies, or, perhaps, to those who've fallen prey to evil, old-fashioned, "religious" influences. They may have known only Sad Young Men from the Boys in the Band generation.

Careful observers will note that these myth manufacturers are prone to mild, almost imperceptible, remarks that denigrate gay inclinations.

What should we think when they spout their negativism? Simply that their choices of companions and, perhaps, of values, have been poor. They've adopted a loser's philosophy, one which is of no good use today. When we brush elbows or any other parts of our anatomy with them, perhaps there is something we can do to revivify their faith in themselves and their fellow men. If not, we should simply move on.

A SIZE-QUEEN'S LOVER

Dear Lige and Jack,

I will start my letter by telling all about myself. My age is twenty-five. I live with my family and they are very rich. I own a small business and make about $15,000 a year for myself. But I'm 5'10'' and 190 pounds and, being on the fat side my cock seems very small, and this has got me upset. I have a boyfriend. He is very good-looking and he has seven and a half inches and he wants me to do oral on him, but he doesn't want to take me orally, as he likes big ones only. But I do love him very much, and when it comes to making out, he is OK.

Please let me know what I should do. Do you think that he is just using me as a cocksucker or do you think we have real love for each other and we should still be friends? He is the only guy that I can say that I have really loved. If we were to stop being friends, where could I start looking for someone to give my love to? I think that I should start looking for new friends. I think that the right guy would understand that love is more important than the size of my cock, right?

Send me a letter as soon as you can. I hope that you can be of some help to me.

Sincerely,
Foster H.
Irvington, New Jersey

Dear Foster,
Luckily you've realized that the size of your cock isn't important, or, if it is important, it is so to people with starched values. Also, you're on the verge of realizing that it's time for you to make new friends. New friends are always an adventure!

There's no reason why you shouldn't continue to hit it off smooching with your boyfriend, but if he's a "size queen," move on at the same time to greener pastures where there are people who appreciate you for the warmth of your touch, the relaxed, carefree abandon of your body and most of all, because you make them feel they're in the presence of someone they trust.

To develop these traits you may need more experience. Judging by your letter we'd say that your sexual experience has been somewhat limited. Open the doors of your body to pleasure from many different angles.

Being on the chubby side, you'd be wise to take a sincere interest in caring for your body and the result, even if you don't lose a lot of weight, would at least be better posture, an easygoing manner, and self-awareness. Your individuality will shine and people will find you more attractive.

•

AN ERECTION IS THE PROBLEM

Dear Lige and Jack,
I am twenty-two years old and am considered a good-looking man. I have a problem I would like to talk over with you. Maybe you can help.

I am in the U.S. Navy and will be leaving Oct. 29th; this will be my four years completed in service.

I'm stationed in Scotland now.

My problem is sex. I've had opportunity with many women here but I have trouble getting an erection. I feel sometimes that I'm not a whole man and maybe I should turn to homosexuality.

Is there anything I can take? Or should I see a doctor? This is a serious matter to me.

I'm kind of embarrassed writing this but I need advice.

I've had intercourse once in my life. I've also tried other things with a male companion, but that didn't help either.

I hope I've explained this right.

Sincerely,
Ron C.

Dear Ron,
You've had sexual intercourse once, right? It can happen again. Think back and consider what made it possible the first time. Maybe you felt a more direct connection to the girl. Perhaps she was really attractive to you in some very important ways and that's why you turned on to her. Or, if it was just a quickie

35

affair, nothing too important, it's possible that you simply lost your self-consciousness about sex.

Part of your approach to sexuality is evident in your letter. Don't seek sexual relationships—with men or women—because you hope to prove something to yourself. Sexual feelings don't rise with just anybody, you know. Let's face it—you're inexperienced—and you must allow time and circumstance to let your feelings come to the fore naturally. You're trying to force yourself to be excited—regardless of gender—when, it seems, you need to let your mind flow freely and stop being so studious and serious about sex.

Tell your lovers you like to get naked and frolic, but that that doesn't mean you're going to screw. Pretend to be a bit coy. Play with them and examine them. You're a near-virgin, right? Virgins have privileges. Don't take your privileges only with your cock. Take them with your sight, your touch, your taste. Remember the Yellow Pages ad? *Let your fingers do the walking! Slowly. Don't rush.* When you make love don't think about *what's going to happen.* Don't worry about *what just happened* either. Just enjoy what's happening! If this formula doesn't turn you into a winner sooner or later, check with a doc to see if you've got a physical disability.

•

"I WANT TO WEAR A DRESS"

Dear Lige and Jack,

I'm writing to you because you seem to be understanding about transvestites (since one writes for your newspaper).

I am not a transvestite. At least I'm not one yet. But I do have a desire to wear women's clothes. I'm not really interested in

36

men. I like the thought of female things. Therefore, I don't believe I'm gay. But I wonder what I should do about my desire to wear the clothes of the opposite sex.

I'd be afraid to go out in public and I'd almost die of embarrassment trying to buy women's clothes in a department store. But since I've seen that there are other men courageous enough to do it, why shouldn't I?

Do you have any suggestions about what I maybe should do? Thank you for your time spent answering me.

Sincerely,
Juan P.
Miami, Florida

Dear Juan,

You're right in surmising that you're probably not gay. Most transvestites aren't. There's no necessary connection between one's taste in clothes and one's sexual orientation. Most gay men are attracted to men. You are attracted to feminine things.

We know several transvestites who are happily married men with children and grandchildren. Their wives know about them and accept them. They tell us that some of their "straight" transvestite friends would be very much offended if anyone thought they were homosexuals. Of course many people do. It is a mistake common to many gay people as well as to straights. Many don't understand why a "straight" man dresses in women's clothes.

There are, natch, drag queens in the gay world, but they're quite different from transvestites. Usually they're flamboyant and garish. Transvestites are harder to spot when they go out in public. Most don't go out, however, for fear of being arrested or beaten by toughs. These are some of the sadder pressures that transvestites—who hurt no one—must contend with. They upset and freak out the masses. Whatever you do, be careful.

Check with your local gay lib group and ask them to direct you to the transvestite community. Perhaps you can discover more about yourself and what you really want to do.

A preoccupation with clothes and fashions (*outer garments*) is difficult for us to grasp. It seems superficial, and isn't in line with our highest priorities. But if it gives *you* pleasure and fits your values comfortably, then we say "Right on!" It is your business, after all, how you dress. This *should be* a free country and people ought to be able to wear whatever they like. Good luck!

●

LOVECHILE

Dear Lige and Jack,

As a Black person I would like to tell your publication that the constant comparison of the Black or minority oppression with the oppression of you white Homosexuals is an affront and is offensive to Black people. Those few who are crazy enough to buy your publication see nothing but the work of spoiled white sissies who've had their fill of men to the point where they don't know what they want anymore. You white Homos have been catered to for years; you've been glorified in phony physique magazines which nowadays come out with puny white (male) bitches right on the front covers. But that's not enough now. You want the whole world to love you. Well, as far as I'm concerned, you racist cocksuckers can go on getting killed and go straight to Hell. You've got your nerve to use the struggles of Black people to further your sickening, selfish cause when very few, if any, can even relate to Blacks or give a damn about them. I don't care what the Hell you Queers do, but I'm warning you now that you'd better keep Black people out of it.

Kill all white Homos! I hate whites! Kill! Kill! Kill!

M.P.J.
New York City

Dear Love Buds,

How strange that you're so bugged by our sexual preferences. Your scene becomes downright weird since you've let us know you're a constant reader of a gay publication.

In the "gay world" there has perhaps always been a greater degree of friendly association between Blacks and Whites than in most other segments of society. We have experienced discrimination and so, more often than not, many of us react to others in similar positions with understanding and compassion instead of hate. Sexuality cuts across all phony racial lines.

True, there are differences between the Black struggle and the Gay struggle. There are also similarities. Peoples of different skin colors or sexual orientations should realize they have an equal stake in freedom to be themselves without institutionalized interference.

Black *is* Beautiful and Gay *is* Glorious! Dig it.

●

NUDIE-BOOK CRITIC

Dear Lige and Jack,

Am I wrong in thinking that all I see is white nudes in most gay publications?

I'm emotionally hurt and it makes me a little mad when I see that white is quite bright in publications and motion pictures for gays. It's ridiculous to see just white skins in front of my brown eyes.

Black and Gay
Elwood C.
New York City

Dear Elwood,
Why don't you send protest letters to the nudie-book publishers and carbon copies of those letters to every major gay publication. Let the nudie-book publishers know you're gunning for them by telling them you've sent the carbons. It helps.

Funny, the nudie books we've seen usually contain at least a few photos of black men. But then we've found that spending too much time with nudie books keeps us from coming face to face with real men.

Nudie books are hardly ever representative of the best in gay culture. You get pissed because the models are all white. Fine. But we get pissed because they all look so stupid. Like hustlers, plucked from the bus station. Not that there's something wrong with all bus station hustlers. It's just that most of them try to have sex with their legs crossed, many are violent, and it's always wise to hide your wallet. Inspiring, they are not.

•

BLACK AND GAY

Dear Lige and Jack,
To those people who are Black and Gay (and the number is not small) there must inevitably be an ultimate moment as to which

to be first, Black or Gay. This dilemma will undoubtedly cause multiple changes to occur in the heads of not only those who fill both descriptions, but in the heads of those who are Black and in the heads of those who are Gay.

For those who are both, there must be a personal assessment as to whether or not your love life will be affected by which you choose to be first. It should be remembered that you were Black long before you were Gay; however (except in cases of the severely uptight), it can be safely assumed that you would rather screw than rally. It is because you belong to two minority groups that it is mandatory for you to get your head together as soon as possible. Don't let your mental standpoint be shaken by people screaming "Homosexuality Made Me a Nigger." The hell with that. This writer has been Black for many moons (and Gay for a few moons too!) and I can't remember being a nigger once. And if anybody should know if you're a nigger—it's you. Who was it that said that you have to be Black to be a nigger in the first place? Watch out baby, or society will poison your brain.

The choice of who you make it with is still up to you—but you have to have your head together on both fronts before you can really enjoy it whoever it is. Nobody will twist your arm to bang the sheets (liberation isn't quite that widespread yet); but also, nobody will restrict you from humping who you please. There are sufficient numbers of Gays to continually ring your chimes whether you dig Blacks or Whites or both.

Granted that there are many Gays both Black and White who have developed a definite love of interracial nookie. Exclusively. Conversely, there are Gays both Black and White who only dig other Black and White (respectively) Gays. Somewhere in the middle (why is the majority always in the middle?) are the Gays who dig both.

Think about the whole thing slowly. There are a lot of humpy Blacks stomping the streets, a lot of humpy Whites, humpy

Puerto Ricans, humpy Orientals. You can take the whole or any part thereof. Whatever moves you. The choice is yours. Militancy should not dictate how you get your rocks off. If your head says be separate—solid! Someone will be glad to lose the competition, and someone else will mourn their loss. Six of one, a half dozen of the other.

Don't mix politics with sex—especially Gay sex. There's enough shit in your head already. Think about one thing at a time. Think Black. Think Gay. Then think both and decide which you will devote the most energy to. The battle to be Gay and free is almost identical to the battle to be Black and free. Being Gay is not a sickness, just as being Black is not a curse. Gay is good and Black is beautiful. People are finally just beginning to get the message. But both fronts need every voice available. Get your head together, Honey—Nobody'll care who you love.

> Love (or a more accessible substitute),
> Phillip H.
> New York City

Dear Phillip,
You are beautiful and there's no bout adout it!

•

FROM ST. PAUL, JR.

Dear Sirs,
What's so joyous about being gay? Jesus Christ offers more joy. He said, "Whoever believeth in me and obeys me shall not perish but have life everlasting." Being gay is not entertaining.

I can get more entertainment by reading the Bible, praying, speaking the word of God, playing baseball, basketball, football. Jesus says: "No man can get to the Father except through me." The gay world isn't the only world. If you go to the Lord you can be much happier and you won't be sad. Men do shameful things with each other and because of this wrongdoing they deserve punishment.

The Lord shall not abandon the good when the bad want to hurt them. The only way you can be well balanced is by believing in Christ because then you will be less nervous.

There is nothing funny about this. It is true. I don't think you should tell people it's OK to be gay. It is dirty. It is no good influencing young children to do it. Older people should help eighteen-year-olds, etc. Don't hurt them. Remember when you die I told you this. When God tells you that it is wrong and you persist, you're going to hell. Christ said, "I am the bread of life." How can you liberate when you are not mature enough? If you were matured enough you'd turn to Christ instead.

> Yours in God,
> New York, New York

Dear Baseball-Playing, Basketball-Playing Bible Reader,
You say "There's nothing funny about this." Quite truthfully, we weren't laughing. If your belief makes you less nervous, we are glad. We wish you good faith!

Our view of Christ is not a Fundamentalist's however. We do not believe that love and affection between two people, no matter what their gender, can possibly be dirty. The "Christ" to whom we turn is not a mere historical figure but a divine reality which exists in every person, no matter what his or her religious beliefs may be.

We would advise people to look inward for "Christ"—to

"the light within," rather than seeking him in so-called holy books and scriptures. Read lots of books—not only the Bible—and if they don't satisfy you, get out in some lovely park and play more baseball.

● ● ●

ANTI-GAY CRUSADERS

Anti-homosexual moralizers—particularly the loud ones—are motivated by vague fears and self-deprecation caused by their own psychological struggles to suppress and hide various homosexual impulses in themselves. These are the people who insist that homosexuality will become rampant and will spread if gay people aren't sent back to their closets. They fail to realize that such arguments are tacit admissions that such impulses are innate in all mankind.

It is in a man's relationships with other gay people that the destructive nature of anti-homosexual prejudice does truly vile damage. A person can't live in pretense, covering his feelings at every turn and enduring callous slurs from unsuspecting relatives and friends without its having far-reaching effects on his personality.

When he starts a relationship with another gay person in which there's a mutual sharing of life and love, he often questions himself incessantly. Is the union moral? Is it right? Does it really have value? He may not have been able to muster the enormous strength that's often required to buck social norms. He may dislike himself—perhaps unconsciously—for having entered into such a relationship and frequently may punish himself in bizarre ways for doing so.

Like all people who put the blame for their discomforts on the handiest "culprit," this man blames homosexuality, thinking there may be something inherent in its nature that causes him to mismanage his life. Such an attitude destroys with a vengeance since there's nothing he can do to rid himself of his impulses; hence he will carry guilt and self-damnation to his grave.

IF THE GOVERNMENT
BUGS YOUR BED?

Attn: Lige and Jack,
This is in regard to your article on the Pentagon, and a booklet mentioned, which was entitled ''What To Do In Case of a Federal Interrogation.''
If possible, could you please tell me where I might appropriate this booklet?

Sincerely,
Elliott H.
Tampa, Florida

Dear Elliott,
We are enclosing a copy of ''What to Do In Case of a Federal

45

Interrogation." It was composed by a well-known gay liberationist, Dr. Franklin E. Kameny of Washington, D.C.:

"The discriminatory policies of the Federal Government in disqualifying the homosexual citizen from Federal employment, from eligibility for a security clearance, and from service in and fully honorable discharge from the Armed Forces, are not only unjustified, but are gravely injurious to the national interest. It is, therefore, the patriotic duty of every American citizen to do everything lawfully within his power to impede and to obstruct the implementation of these policies, and to encourage others to do likewise. Central to that implementation is the conduct of investigations involving the administration of interrogations. To those finding themselves subjected to such interrogations, the following pointers and suggestions are offered.

SAY NOTHING; SIGN NOTHING; GET COUNSEL; FIGHT BACK

"1. No citizen is required to submit to an interrogation by any Federal official—F.B.I., Civil Service Commission, military investigators, etc.—or even to speak to them. However, in certain instances (for example, where you yourself, rather than an acquaintance, are the subject of the investigation), it may be advisable to grant to the Government the privilege of interviewing you.

"Any interrogation, interview, or discussion held in the absence of Counsel, which lasts longer than *10 seconds* has lasted too long. Use the 10 seconds to obtain the investigator's name and official phone number so your Counsel can contact him later. *THEN TERMINATE THE INTERVIEW—AT ONCE*.

"2. In case of such interrogation, your choice is *not* between telling truth or untruth, but between speaking and not speaking. Never lie, falsify, or misrepresent. On matters relating to

46

homosexuality—yours or anyone else's—just refuse to speak.

"Put your own judgment as to what should or should not be said into deep-freeze cold-storage, and simply keep quiet. There is just simply *NO* valid excuse—*NONE*—for providing government interrogators with ANY information—ANY. Anything that you *do* say should be meticulously true, as far as it goes, but nothing should be said.

"3. If you are asked any questions at all on homosexuality, in any aspect, your *only* answers should be: 'These are matters which are of no proper concern to the Government of the United States under any circumstances whatever,' and 'This is information which the Government does not have the need to know.' Stand your ground on these. Do not engage in philosophical or psychological or sociological discourses. Do not make use of the Fifth Amendment to the Constitution; it is not necessary, and may be harmful.

"4. Sign no statements; take no lie-detector tests; give no names or other information about any other person.

"Do not try to defend yourself; do not try to provide excuses or explanations; do not try to correct inaccuracies, no matter how terrible their information and accusations sound; do not affirm or deny anything, true or untrue. All of that can be done much more effectively later on. *JUST SHUT UP*.

"In the last analysis, most governmental cases are made out of the individual's own mouth. If you keep your mouth tightly shut and keep your pen in your pocket, they are likely to be unable to make a case that will stick, legally, and you will avoid endless grief for yourself and others.

"This advice applies, as well, to so-called 'psychiatric evaluations.' They should be terminated *at once,* before this 'talk machinery' has been started.

"5. Under no circumstances tolerate unannounced visitations by investigators at your home or your place of employ-

47

ment. Refuse to speak to them; insist upon a proper appointment, at a time and place of *your* choice and convenience. *Insist* upon the right to be accompanied by one or more persons of your choice (without restriction to professional legal counsel) to act not only as counsel, but as witness.

"6. The interrogators will try to cajole, to persuade, to bully, to demand, to threaten, to bargain. Do not be taken in. Regardless of what they may say and how they may act, they are "out to get you." Among a few of their favorite techniques are:

a. You are not cooperating. Of course you are not. You have no reason to cooperate. Continue not to.

b. All of this is not really very important, and nothing will happen to you; we just need a few questions answered and your signature, so we can complete our records and close our files. Don't believe it.

c. The laws or regulations require you to reply. This is not true, regardless of what may be quoted to you or even shown to you in print.

d. The good guy and bad guy approach. After interrogator A has unpleasantly browbeaten you for a while, interrogator B will intercede, supposedly as your friend, to try to make things easier for you, and to modify interrogator's A attitude. Do not be taken in. They are both your enemies.

"7. This is stated with very strong overemphasis, because extensive experience has shown that without it, this advice, as simple as it is, is not properly heeded: On matters having in any way to do with homosexuality, say NOTHING; no-thing means NO thing; and no means NONE AT ALL, with NO exceptions. It does NOT mean just a little. This means that you do NOT discuss juvenile homosexual experiences, and you do NOT discuss so-called passive acts, or anything else at all. You say NOTHING whatever. Do not attempt to exercise your judgment as to what may or may not be harmful to discuss. Close the door

48

firmly and absolutely to discussion or comment upon *any* and every aspect of homosexuality and, in fact, of sex generally.

"8. Do not confirm information which they allegedly have. They may not have what they have led you to believe they have, and they may be only guessing or deducing. Even if there is no doubt as to their possession of information, you will be better off if there has been no confirmation or corroboration from you.

"9. Insist that you be treated with the full respect and dignity due *all* American citizens in every status, by *all* their public servants, at *all* levels, at *all* times. If you are not so treated, walk out and do not return until you have received, in writing, an apology for past improper treatment, and assurances of future proper behavior. If you receive no such apology, object, by letter, to the appropriate Cabinet-level official, with details of the behavior and language involved, and inform your local gay liberation organization.

"10. Remember that the information involved in investigations is classified, as far as the Government is concerned. If anyone—particularly including your employer—is informed by anyone but you of the subject or any details of an investigation of you, you can bring criminal charges against the investigators or other officials who have discussed the information. Do so. At the same time, do not allow yourself to be misled into believing that you are not permitted to discuss any and all aspects of the matter with anyone you choose. You may seek counsel and advice from anyone and are completely free to discuss all aspects of the matter with persons of your own choice, at all times.

"11. Do not resign and do not allow yourself to be stampeded into a resignation: you must be given a reasonable amount of time to make a decision. Contest, first administratively and then in the courts, as high as need be, all firings, less than fully honorable discharges, and security-clearance denials based upon homosexuality. To the fullest extent possible, challenge not the mere allegations of fact, but the policies, laws and regulations involved.

"Do not worry about the attitudes of the investigators toward you, or about creating hostility or antagonism on their part, or about 'what it will look like' if you do not cooperate. Their attitudes, and such appearances, are totally irrelevant. What determines your fate (or that of someone else—friend, acquaintance, etc., about whom you may be questioned) is the actual *information*—the *facts*—which do or do not get into the record. That comes—or does not come—out of your mouth. See to it that NO information comes out of your mouth. Information—accurate or inaccurate—already on the record can be dealt with far more effectively later on. Do not attempt to deal with it at the interrogation or interview level. *Just shut up!*

The entire transmission of information at such governmental interview should be *to* you *from* the interviewers, not the other way round.

"By following the advice above, you will be serving not only your own best interests and those of your acquaintances and fellow citizens, but the best interests of your country.

"Gay liberation organizations will be pleased to offer coaching, advice and encouragement to those good citizens who wish lawfully to impede their government's ill-advised efforts to disqualify homosexuals—reducing them, thereby, to second-class citizenship, to the loss of all citizens."

•

A SHRINK'S TWANG

Dear Lige and Jack,
My psychiatrist, who is from Vienna, and has all the degrees

you need, and diplomas, plus a big twang, says he doesn't really like Americans socially—he says they're really a bit facetious.

He says he likes them sexually (or "suckshually") but that socially they're a bit of a drag. (Actually I think he's a little crazy, but with his twang, who cares!)

Anyway, when he's not letting me swing on his big twang, he's advising me on current suck mores, and he says it's OK now to say you're one and also to let down both your hair and your pants when you're in a compatible suck group.

Actually I object to his overuse of the word suck, but really, with his big twang, who cares!

And he told me not to suck so hard (on his big twang) because I could develop like a Viennese complex.

He also said Vienna was never like this!

Yussi D.
New York City

Dear Yussi,
Your shrink sounds one-dimensional. Ask him to turn over.

It's nice to know what established psychiatrists are doing on their couches these days! At least you're getting *something* for your money.

● ● ●

20th CENTURY WITCHDOCTORS

Gay people who go to psychiatrists—accepting society's moral dictates—are often treated over a long time span for a nonexistent illness.

At great expense and sacrifice these poor women and men make heroic attempts to square their sexual feelings with conventional demands. They believe, for some strange reason, that sexual uniformity is a necessity for happiness and sexual diversity should be frowned upon.

When they find themselves still unable to change after many years of therapy, their doctors excuse their own failures by telling them that they unconsciously do not want to change and that they're using therapy as a "cover-up" to ease their consciences.

Such doubletalk, passed in the name of "science," cannot be lightly excused. It is not only medical quackery but a new level of foul play. A psychiatrist accepts money for the proposed "cure" of a state of being which has never been shown to be a sickness.

Psychiatrists and psychoanalyists are as united or as disunited as any group of theorists. (One might compare them with philosophers and theologians.) It is well known that Freud's able pupils Adler and Jung disagreed with their master and set up their own schools of thought. What is not well known, however, is that there is such an enormous variety of opinion among shrinks that Robert A. Harper was able to write a book in 1959 called *Psychoanalysis and Psychotherapy: 36 Systems*. Since then the number of new systems—including such recent plebeian developments as primal therapy and transactional analysis—has doubled the total.

Psychiatry's failure to meet the needs of the homosexual in America is a tale of bureaucratic skullduggery with overtones of dog-eat-dog capitalism.

Until quite recently, the American Psychiatric Association has refused to reconsider its loony, longstanding position: that homosexuality, per se, is, in psychiatric nomenclature, a pathological condition. On March 21, 1973, the

52

official newspaper of the APA carried an announcement on its front page which said that the New England Psychiatric Society, a branch of the APA representing 650 psychiatrists in Massachusetts and New Hampshire, was calling for an end to legal and employment discrimination against homosexuals and of legal restrictions on sexual acts of consenting adults. More importantly, the New England group also stated: "Present evidence indicates that many homosexuals are functioning in a way that cannot be considered an illness." Hallelujah! At last the shrinks were coming around.

Two months later a thousand assembled psychiatrists met at the annual American Psychiatric Association convention in Honolulu, Hawaii. They listened to panelists debate "Should Homosexuality Be in the American Psychiatric Nomenclature?"—in other words, whether or not homosexuality should be kept on their list of sicknesses.

How, in Freud's name, did they ever classify homosexuality as a sickness in the first place? Any fool can plainly see that as a human condition, homosexuality has only one symptom: attraction to a person of the same sex.

The psychiatrists and so-called psychotherapists, more than any other organized group, have been enemies of the homosexual community. Their names are legion: Bergler, Bieber, Ellis, Hatterer, Socarides and Cappon. All of these men have crusaded actively to make life for homosexually inclined people as difficult as possible. Charles Socarides, for example, once recommended a "national treatment center" to which all homosexuals would be sent. Socarides was frequently a witness for the U.S. Government in cases when the Government wished to fire a known homosexual employee. Socarides would drop in on the trial and testify that the "homosexual condition" is

53

psychopathic. The government would pay him generously for doing so. Such a dear sweet man. A healer. We noted with interest that he was among those arguing for the status quo at the American Psychiatric Association's Honolulu convention.

Treatment received by gay men at the hands of orthodox therapists has been depressing indeed. Instead of helping them to question a moronic social structure, these headshrinkers have tried to eliminate or to change their sexual orientations to suit grandparents, an approach which has been universally recognized as a dismal failure.

Why must establishment psychiatrists encourage adherence to values in vogue? Most shrinks have allowed their gay patients to assume that society's mores are A-OK and that any faults lie in the patient himself. Instead of bolstering self-confidence, the psychiatrist has been in the lucrative business of destroying it, thereby keeping his more affluent clients in tow indefinitely.

The psychiatric tradition has encouraged the view that one's homosexual feelings are a loathesome social burden. Those who've been influenced by this tradition have hidden their feelings, felt guilty about them, and have suffered a loss of self-confidence. The shrinks have promoted a bizarre distraction with the *object* of a patient's affection. "It's not *how* you love," they say, "but *whom* you love." We disagree.

• • •

LONGING FROM AFAR

Dear Lige and Jack,

Ten years I have lived in the same neighborhood with a Black Gay. We live so near; only four doors away, yet so far apart. He is beautiful and very Black and so very Gay, and knows it very well. I feel that I too is equally his contender in these fields of our unique human nature. And still we do not recognize each other as being equal with two dynamic individual personalities which has so much in common.

For the same ten years we have walked past and hungrily searched into the depths of one another's eyes. Still not a word have passed our tormented lips.

I have now entered my first year of medical college, but sorrowfully, he dropped out of school while in the tenth grade. Reasons being: the ignorance and stupidity of the students, fore they lacked insight of him as being a totally different person than they could possibly conceive.

Through rumors from our not so understanding peers I know that he is taking voice lessons for a career. But this is not the problem. The problem lies in the desire that we entensely share for one another. I sometimes wonder if this problem would exist if it were not for the fact that we don't differ in that of our feelings but only in that of our skin pigmentation. Fore, you see, he is a beautiful Black Gay and I, White.

Is it so impossible to overcome this barrier, if we share equal love and desire for one another. We talk of one another to strangers but we talk not to each other. Can we break the barrier that society have manifested in our minds as a dease [*disease*] and if so, how long?

When will the silence be broken, and how do one go about it?

Sincerely yours,
Johnny
Philadelphia, Pennsylvania

55

Dear Johnny,

We suspect that *you* are the beautiful Gay dropout and your intended one is the White fellow who's in his first year of medical school. No matter, except that you shouldn't have tried to hide the fact that you're Black by reversing the situation in your letter. Enjoy your dark skin! Realize how beautiful it is! Learn to be proud of your Blackness and when you are, you can pass your friend on the street and smile. Say hello. Be friendly. The most terrible barriers in the world can be jumped when you grin from ear to ear and offer a stranger your hand.

● ● ●

DIVERSITY

No two anythings are exactly alike. Blades of grass, fingerprints, trees and sexual feelings all differ. Inexhaustible diversity is nature's pattern.

Nearly all people fear death, but to abandon the right to be one's self—no matter how different—is to die.

To long to be like others is to glorify imitation. The worst thing about imitating is that most people imitate whatever is commonplace. They exchange their actual selves for what is known as reputation. It is a despicable trade. How terrible to feel indebted to others for everything one has become, and to sense that one's self has no real substance of its own.

● ● ●

A SCARY SKINFLICK

Dear Lige and Jack,
I seem to recall reading a gay movie review you wrote at one time. It would be helpful if you regularly reviewed these flesh flicks, as an information service. I mention this because of one such film I recently saw. The title, *Brushed Angel*, should have raised my suspicions. The "Angel," a white guy with an Afro style hairdo, which completely turned me off, was subjected to such "erotic" tortures as having the head of his penis burnt with a lit cigarette by a supposed transvestite (who turned me further off.) He endured apparently painful, sharply twisted skin sensations, as clothespins were ripped off his legs, chest and nipples. Besides, the transvestite's large uncircumsized pointed redheaded cock was most unappetizing. I watched for a half hour then left in disgust. Reviews, giving such details as I have herein, would preclude customers' throwing their money away.

Sincerely,
Denny T.
New York City

Dear Denny,
Quite right, unless you happen to be a sadistic transvestite with a large uncircumsized pointed redheaded cock.

•

STARS IN HIS EYES

Dear Lige and Jack:
Having long read your contribution to the gay press and finding your viewpoints informative, clear and well directed, I'm

a bit alarmed at your recent blanket put-down of astrology.

My interest in astrology has been deep enough to involve me in studying and drawing charts for eight years. I've avidly read a couple of serious astrology monthlies as well as following star trends and I might state that astrology scholars disagree and debate many points. However the only reference to homosexuality that I've run across is in the July 1966 issue of *American Astrology*. I quote:

> Homosexuality must be considered as both a natural and abnormal phenomenon. Natural because in its broadest sense everything which exists in nature is that. Abnormal because it contravenes the prevailing moral standards of most societies and their commonly held conception of a particular physiological function in nature vital to the continuation of life itself.

There follows in this article (by Robert R. Shanks) a number of astrological formations which he correlated from a study of horoscopes of diverse admitted homosexuals and could only be comprehended by someone with a great knowledge and understanding of astrology. It's hardly a put-down of homosexuality nor as uncomplicated as "the wrong planets getting mixed up," etc. In fact certain signs of exaltation (the highest order of the right planets) are implicated in this particular article.

Incidently, as no horoscope is exactly the same for any person, for over 300 years, astrology is a profound affirmation of the individuality of each living being. As anyone should know, homosexuality can occur under any star, although as the stars give certain people more sensuality or sexual drive than others, more sexual persons will experiment with sexual variations. In concluding, I would like to add that the horoscopes of two people involved in any sexual union determine more than one individual horoscope, and the stars that determine an aberration in one horoscope do not necessarily determine the same aberration in another. "The stars impel. They do not compel."

Claude P.
New York City

Dear Claude,
Thank goodness astrologers have developed a softer, more humane rap on the whole gay question. Like priests and ministers, no doubt, they're discovering that ten percent of the adult population can't be ignored without risking severe economic setbacks.

If you choose to run your life by looking at astrology charts, who are we to object? It's in your stars!

•

ALONE IN OMAHA

Dear Lige and Jack,
As I have nowhere else to turn I am writing to you. I am a lonely young man, slowly reaching the point of desperation. So far I've found nowhere to fit in.

I will shortly be returning to Omaha again to enter into the study of law and business. I'm too rushed with studies to complain, but it would be much easier if I, at least, had just one person to write to during that period.

My most urgent desire when I have the summer off is to find an occupation that will place me in the midst of my kind.

I've considered Los Angeles or San Francisco, but know of

59

no one to write to to learn of permanant or summer employment.

Whatever talents I have are languishing where I'm now residing. If only I had friends and employment. Please heed me. You're all I have left to to turn for help. Any information will be unendingly appreciated.

> With affection,
> Mark J.
> St. Charles, Missouri

Dear Mark,
Your loneliness isn't unique.

If you can't find any gay friends why not just make friends! There are lots of lonely people besides yourself no matter where you are. Don't weep for yourself. Help someone else who is lonely. That's what gay liberation is all about. Those who need friendship don't have to be gay!

If you go to the West Coast, there are hundreds of gay nightclubs and bars in San Francisco and Los Angeles. Check with your local gay organizations there about jobs and ask about the friendliest night spots.

But before you go anywhere, understand one fact: the people you call "your kind" are as varied as the people who aren't your kind. Don't be a leaner. When you move, you don't need old friends to depend on. Make *new* friends when you arrive. If you need a pen pal, put an ad for one in the personals columns of the gay tabloids. All sorts of "your kind" will send you everything from thoughtful, romantic proposals to gloriously filthy letters.

● ● ●

LOOK TO THIS DAY!

Becoming a happy person hasn't nearly as much to do with the events of one's *past* life (with the treatment received at the hands of Mom and Dad or whatever other reverie into which some shrink may try to sucker a patient) but with acting *now* as though the past is nonexistent, seeing what we can do *now* to improve our lives. Robert Ingersoll had the right idea:

> We waste no time in useless dread,
>   In trembling fear;
> The present lives, the past is dead,
>   and we are here,
> All welcome guests at life's great feast

And centuries ago, Indian mystics saluted the dawn by singing:

> Look to this day!
> For yesterday is but a dream
> And tomorrow is only a vision,
> But every day well lived
> Makes every yesterday a dream of happiness
> And every tomorrow a vision of hope.

Although we never receive letters asking "What causes my homosexuality?" we've noted in conversation with the (gay) man in the street that this is still something of an unspoken concern, a hangover, probably, from psychiatric propaganda. Even in up-to-date dissertations, such as pseudonymous John Reid's humorous tale of his "coming out," (*The Best Little Boy in the World*) there is a morbid preoccupation with "causation" or "what made me this

61

way?" "There is nothing predictive in what I'm saying," writes Reid, "except perhaps to the extent that there may be a greater *probability*, if still a fairly small one, that short people with funny names, or tall people without fathers, or medium people who were overly sheltered will turn out to be gay."

Behind the question of "causation" lies the veiled assumption that there is something *wrong* with homosexual inclinations. No one ever asks "What caused your heterosexuality?" because that particular orientation is taken for granted. It might be somewhat startling, for example, if we were to suggest that "straight" desires were *caused* possibly because a man's sexual development hadn't been arrested in time.

A homosexual person's engrossment in "causation" covers, rather imperfectly, a host of often defensive feelings. His uncertainty about the propriety of his sex life, triggered by society's overt hostility, can create a lack of easygoing self-approval.

If scientific inquiries are to be made about causation, the more important question is *what causes sexual orientation?* Phrased this way, there can be no hint of prejudgment, no onus. Meanwhile, on the personal level, it is wise to drop this question as totally irrelevant against the backdrop of our larger inquest: how can we be happy in the here and now?

• • •

A PRISON RECORD

Dear Sirs,
I was just released from prison after serving three years. Now that I'm out I don't know what to do with myself. I came out in prison and therefore have never been to a gay bar, a club, bath or anything. I don't want to make an ass of myself due to my inexperience. I do want to meet other gay people though, but want them to like me. How should I act? Should I tell them about my prison record?

> Yours truly,
> Hershel Lee H.
> Waco, Texas

Dear Hershel,
Gay people act pretty much like everyone else. A little experience will teach you do's and don'ts. Act honestly.

Your prison record shouldn't prove to be a big deal to folks worth knowing. It's not necessary to go about labeling yourself an ex-con, though. If the subject comes up, don't be ashamed. It's been part of your life, after all. But concern yourself with *today*, not yesterday, and your tomorrow will be happier by far.

● ● ●

FIRST TIME OUT ON THE TOWN

A man's first journey into the gay subculture is often an occasion for anxiety. His mind registers dangers, real and imagined, although mostly the latter, if he makes the proper preparations.

Anyone from the boondocks who is new to city life should obtain a gay guide to the city he's visiting. It would be wise to pay visits to local gay organizations, specifying that one is new to the city experience and would appreciate help in getting oriented.

The greatest difficulties usually come to those who are unacquainted with the locations of gay sites. In most cities the homosexual community is generally peaceful and law abiding and there are always plenty of fun spots to visit. On the other hand, there are always locales where the naive face hazards—male prostitutes, disgruntled police and other questionable characters are quick to take advantage of those with little know-how.

Once familiar with a region a man should experience few troubles, and usually much sooner than later will find himself surrounded by new friends and acquaintances. Newcomers should realize, however, that the gay people they meet are not, as conventional society has taught them to think, interested only in sex. It's a common misconception among the unsophisticated that any gay person will "get it on" with anybody, just as long as they happen to be of the same sex. This, of course, is nonsense.

An inexperienced man who is searching for new friends should expect them to behave in much the same way that people *everywhere* behave. He should understand that sexuality is not the motivating factor in gay relationships any more than in straight ones.

Some newcomers can easily be spotted in gay circles because of their approaches to others. Their leers smack of a certain awkward lasciviousness that springs from socially induced delusions about what the gay experience is all about. Generally those with more experience are tolerant of these fresh faces but such artless behavior isn't likely to help them score.

Openness, friendliness, an easygoing smile and a relaxed manner are far more effective during a debut than a serious, determined, sex-starved bearing.

MONEY BAGS

Gentlemen,
I, like you, am gay and I got to wondering if I could meet both of you for the purpose of making love.

Would there be a fee? If so, how much would it be?
Could you come out here?

Sincerely yours,
Donald C.
Old Greenwich, Connecticut

Dear Donald,
Both of us at once would certainly be too much for you. Even so, we wouldn't dream of charging you a fee unless, of course, you're a millionaire and even then we'd have dire pangs of conscience.

We always get lost in Connecticut. Why don't you visit the big city? There are lots of gay men around here who won't charge you a dime. Lots of night spots and hot spots! Pick up a gay guide on almost any Manhattan newsstand. Who knows —maybe our paths will cross someday. We'll be looking for you. Toodle-ooo!

•

ONE TIMER

Dear Sirs,
Could you tell me the best way to meet someone for a lasting friendship? I have tried several ways but they all end up as one-time meetings. They never show up the next time. I may say that I live in a small town and have to go someplace else to look as everyone knows me where I live. Even the ads I have answered and run myself have been useless. If you could give some advice, I would thank you.

Jerome V.
Suffolk, Virginia

Dear Jerome,
Your first meeting with someone can easily be turned into a second meeting and a third meeting (and so forth) when you emit the right kind of vibes.

Since you live in a small town, we'd guess that your experience hasn't been wide, and since you worry about your towns-folk "knowing," perhaps part of your overcautious attitude is unconsciously expressed to others as nervousness and furtiveness and you find it difficult to be the warm personality you know you can be under the best circumstances.

It's possible too that the guys you meet in nearby towns are often as cautious and nervous as you are. Hence, meeting these people can bring about mutual negative reinforcements—you make each other nervous, hunching around so.

Ads are seldom the best way to strike up long-term relationships. Quite often the people who place them are isolated and somewhat socially inept. You need to meet people face to face. Ads can be advantageous for those who seek pen pals, however.

Maybe you need to spend more time in a bigger city where you can meet a variety of people who'll teach you to "hit it off," well on the first meetings. Practice helps. Other men admire independence, self-awareness, relaxation and easygoing humor. Learn from new relationships how to laugh, tell stories and to be direct and honest with new friends. You'll find that they'll want to see you again. Don't expect success on the first round. It takes a while.

•

"22 AND I NEVER EXISTED!"

Dear Lige and Jack:
How should I begin? I'm twenty-two years old, but I feel like I've never existed. I live in a small town, population approximately 2700. I graduated from high school in '69, went to our community college and majored in Business Management. I work as a teller in one of our valley banks. I like my job, but I feel confused. If I told them I'm homosexual I'm sure I would lose my job.

I read a book, *The Gay Crusaders*, which contained an interview with you. I read and reread it and each time I found things I'd missed before. It set me to thinking. How should I put it? I guess it would be all right to say that I want to come out. I'm tired of being closed away, afraid to do anything, say anything,

I want to come out, but how? I don't want to hurt my family. I think I could tell my mother, but she would take it rather hard. I don't have to worry about my father. He's been dead since I was fifteen. But I have four brothers. I'm the youngest one. Actually three are half brothers. My full brother knows I'm gay but I don't think the others would accept me if they knew.

You know, there's one person I've been able to trust. She lives across the street and I can talk to her. She tells me she can't really understand but she accepts me and she says that she hopes I find someone that I could care about.

I hope you don't mind my writing, but I thought that just letting someone else know about me would make me feel just a little better. But if I could I would like to be able to be with people like myself. If I knew how to go about it, maybe I would be able to do something about it.

> Very truly yours,
> Name withheld
> Pennsylvania

Dear Isolated,

Your isolation is an experience common to many who live in small towns, most of whom feel they live under the microscopes of their neighbors.

Take an occasional weekend jaunt to a metropolis. It might not hurt to actually spend a couple of years in a larger town, one of the nation's cleaner cities, where you may wander in those delightful but rare neighborhoods inhabited by compassionate sophisticates who either don't give a hoot about the "carryings-on" behind their neighbor's bedroom doors, or, if they do, it's because they'd like to be behind those doors with the neighbor himself.

Coming out doesn't necessarily mean you must tell others, although by doing so, you're often making it easier to accept your own development. The most important thing for your mother to grasp is that you are a happy person. If she can pick up on that vibe, what she discovers won't hurt her nearly as much. If she's to know, make sure you can take time (years) to educate her and that you know how to do so.

An important part of coming out is learning to understand people who have strong sexual prejudices: not to be too demanding of them. Try to determine how much they're capable of understanding. Never lie about yourself and don't live a "cover-up" life. It's a bore.

•

LONELY

Dear Sirs,
Please print this. Maybe someone, somewhere might understand how I feel.

You see, I'm the only gay person in this rotten town and it's getting me down. Every time I walk up the street, those so-called humans call me names I dare not print on paper, and it hurts me real deep.

I feel like ending it all but I keep up my hope and faith that someday someone will fall in love with me.

I can't even go out at night and cruise for fear I'll get the shit beat out of me. If you know of anyone else who is lonely and would like to write to me please give him my address.

Yours truly,
Doug M.
New Jersey

Dear Doug,

Jeepers! You'll find it hard to be attractive if you go around feeling your town is "rotten." Don't mope. You've got the "small-town blues."

It's true that small-town neighbors—when they discover about young bachelors what they ought to assume, even without asking—they often react with small-town minds. Perhaps you should go where the multitudes swarm . . . where people who don't know each other as well are better Christians and your best dream could be a'waitin'. Learn to like and enjoy yourself more and chances that someone else may fall in love with you will increase one-thousand fold. Names people call you are only simplistic mumblings of barbarians, and if you respect yourself and your feelings, you'll pity them their provincialism.

Visit the largest cities in your locale, pick up gay newspapers and magazines on the newsstands and discover both classifieds for pen pals and lists of places to go where you can live it up!

● ● ●

SMALL-TOWN GOSSIP

What can we say to those who wish to remain in small towns and sparsely populated areas? Isn't it a cop-out to advise such men to move away from their long-time homes to escape suffocating gossip? Gay liberation, after all, must surface in small towns too!

One must appreciate that it's particularly difficult for people who are alive and aware to spend their formative years in small towns. To integrate their personalities, drawing the most from themselves, they must be able to use their varied faculties simultaneously. In small towns there

70

are usually only a very few people, if any, capable of appreciating such people on several levels.

In backwoods areas a young man may risk not only ostracism if it's discovered he's gay but actual threats on his life. This is why we've said to those seeking romance and friendship that they'd be wise to spend time in densely populated areas. In or near large cities they improve their chances for meeting a variety of friends. Gossip becomes tolerable, if not laughable, and there's less personal risk involved, as long as they socialize with people of similar tastes.

A MODEL-TO-BE

Dear Lige and Jack,

I am writing to you because I feel you're the ones who may possibly be able to help me.

I have had an interest in becoming a gay model or even actor in gay films. I would seriously like to make a few films, if possible, or even look into some kind of modeling career. What can you suggest?

I'm 18, good-looking, blond hair, blue eyes, 145 pounds, 5'8'' and average build.

Sincerely,
Wayne S.
Frostburg, Maryland

71

Dear Wayne,

Modeling, which means selling your appearance to commercial concerns for often dubious reasons, is a difficult field for beginners. If you want to break into gay films or be used as a model in gay publications, check the movie ads in gay publications and go straight to the producers of the types of films that interest you, or go directly to the publishers and/or editors of the rags you like and spill your photographs in their laps.

Frankly, although modeling sounds exciting and easy, it's tougher than you'd think. So are some of the plastic-faced models and advertising tycoons you'll have to deal with. If you've got other talents we'd suggest that you use them first and try modeling as a lark after you've developed other ways to sock away some money. Modeling often takes more guts than talent.

•

BALD IS BEAUTIFUL

Dear Lige and Jack,

I am forty-four, active in the gay community, and my attitude toward my own body and soul is positive. But this doesn't much alter the ageist attitudes of others. If I wear a wig to cover my balding grayness, I can be mistaken for a much younger man than I am. When I have done so, the attitudes of others (younger and older) change magically as long as they don't know it's a wig. With or without the wig I am the same person, and just as good in bed. Wearing a wig is a pain in the ass. Why do baldness and grayness, both very male characteristics, suddenly put me in such a frustrating, lonely and sometimes desperate plight.

If I, attractive, balding, graying, slim, attractively muscled forty-four-year-old turned on to you, would you reject me in your search for a young demigod? Or don't you believe in the sensuality and attractiveness of men our age?

Sincerely,
Ralph S.
Los Angeles, California

Dear Ralph,
Of course we wouldn't reject you for such a reason.

Somehow, it seems, you're overly sensitive about baldness. Your beauty comes from within and shows itself in your manner. Many bald men are attractive because they realize this fact.

Wigs are an admission that you find yourself unattractive as you really are. Either of us would turn on more eagerly to a bald man who finds himself attractive than to one who wears a wig.

Perhaps you're associating with men whose values are a bit shallow. What do you think?

Anyway, remember: Bald *is* beautiful! The power of positive thinking creates our realities.

P.S. Let whatever hair you may have do its thing!

• • •

CONSTRUCTIVE NARCISSISM

The practice of self-awareness begins with posture. It is the first necessary step for anyone hoping to improve his self-image and appearance. Good posture is especially needed in today's highly technologized societies which rob our bodies of vitality and self-awareness. Posture also has a profound effect on our balance and mood and shows others how we meet the world. Thus, the quest for a graceful sense of presence.

Correcting posture doesn't mean straightening up, puffing out the chest or squaring the shoulders militarily, at some ridiculous angle.

Finding one's own center of gravity is the process that lies at the core of good posture. It includes an awareness of breathing and is something that can't be mastered in the twinkling of an eye. Posture is an inward feeling for whatever balance means to oneself. Each body expresses it differently, but discovering it requires similar approaches for everyone.

Those who puff their chests, strut arrogantly or hold themselves in exaggerated poses show only that they've missed the essence of posture. Good posture should not be an overstatement or an understatement; not too aggressive and not too passive, but a marvelous centering of the self which includes knowledge of where one is standing *in the present* and how. Whether others notice or not, it is its own reward.

A SADIST'S LOVER YELPS

Dear Lige and Jack,
I've been seeing a guy—who seems like a swell person—for the

last two months. We've been getting along pretty well till now. We're starting to have troubles.

Originally I was attracted to him, I suppose, because he seemed to know where his head was at and he was very masculine and handsome. He wears leather a lot, and he wants me to do the same.

I thought we were getting along fine in bed, but now he's into something different. He wants to tie me to the bed. He likes to pinch my tits and hold me down. He says that it doesn't mean he doesn't dig me, 'cause he does, but he says that behaving like that excites him a lot. Frankly, I was having just as much fun before all this rough stuff started.

One of my best friends says my new lover is a sickie. He seems OK to me, except for this new kick he's getting into. I don't think I should put him down without giving it more of a chance, do you?

Sincerely,
Steve O.
Patterson, New Jersey

Dear Steve,
It's up to you to decide what you want to do with your own mind and body. Don't ask us. But consider this: once you follow a path mixing sexuality and pain, it isn't so easy to return to sexuality as tenderness and pleasure.

What two consenting adults do in bed is their own business. Sadomasochism is a whole different trip. Does it seem altogether joyous and healthy to you?

Sadomashochists can't be defined as "sick." But we would venture to say that most are people with strictly structured psyches. S&M is often a kind of homo-theater in which the director and actor decide in advance what they will and will not

75

do. They also decide what costumes to wear, and exactly what the scene and setting will consist of. Knowing these things in advance provides a kind of security, possibly.

We've often regretted that S&M bars don't feature more dancing, and that there isn't more open laughter, affection, and silliness. It would be nice if there was more variety in the kinds of dress we see in those places too. Don't the patrons ever get tired of wearing motorcycle hats?

But if it's your scene, lover, you're welcome to it. Nobody has a right to tell you you're wrong. Only you can say.

● ● ●

SADOMASOCHISM

S&M is growing rapidly in our culture. Its devotees say that it is a "further step" waiting for those who have grown tired of conventional sex and are looking for new thrills.

No thoughtful person denies that consenting adults have every right to play sadomasochistic games. It is possible, in fact, for long-lasting relationships to take place between sadomasochistic couples, both straight and gay. Since there is a great deal of ignorance about S&M these people often bear the brunt of hostile prejudices.

What we would do, however, is break once and for all the connection between so-called jadedness, said to result from excessive sexual experience, and S&M. We would say to a person who's been encouraged to become a sadomasochist that such a route is not, and need not be, the end product of a wide and growing sexual awareness.

A word which confuses even the "sexually sophisti-

76

cated" is *jadedness*. Precisely what it means is not altogether clear. Ostensibly it refers to being worn out, fatigued, or made weary after a long period of promiscuity. The person thus affected is unable to perform because he has "done everything" and thereafter finds no sexual act gratifying.

The concept of jadedness has little of the validity often attributed to it. While there are certainly people who have had a variety of sexual experiences and subsequently have lost interest in sex except under the most highly specialized circumstances, it is unrealistic to say that too much sexual experience is responsible. In fact it seems that those holding such a theory would oppose an increase of sexual knowledge and experience.

Jadedness is frequently a euphemism for impotence. It provides a man with an ego-protective excuse, namely that his inability to perform is based on too much experience. It is a glamorous excuse for his enfeeblement, since the term casts no aspersion on his virility.

In most cases it is our guess that such impotence has other causes. It can arise, for example, from a rigidly structured view of sexual relations in which each sexual act is experienced and perceived as a distinct deed.

Such mental posturing is extremely inflexible. It bypasses tenderness and concerns itself primarily with physical positioning, hyperconsciousness of each movement as it takes place and focus on certain regular procedures. The sexual act is chopped into categories—fellatio, anal intercourse and other predilections—and is not seen as a flowing whole. Part of this difficulty stems, probably, from puritanical training early in life, woven from the fabric of a sexually retarded society. People who invariably label each sexual movement they make do so because the movements, due to society's negative emphasis on them, seem unprecedented and unique each time they occur. Instead of being accepted as a matter of course, the emphasis returns to these people *consciously* in the midst of sexual passion. This means that they are *self-conscious* and that they see each movement as something *apart* rather than as a passing sequence of spontaneous, playful flux.

Alan Watts said that whenever we command ourselves to get an erection we fail. This is because sexuality is not easily subjected to prearrangements without the loss of the very spontaneity that, for most people, contributes to its excitement. Sexual technique is not nearly as important as attitude and it seems to establish itself without prearrangement when the mind does not concentrate so precisely on what is taking place. Without such concentration the body becomes attuned to a natural rhythm and pulsates uninhibitedly and unselfconsciously.

Sadomasochism is game-oriented. It is practiced by those who concern themselves with controlling and activating mobility in the sex act. Hence, the sadomasochistic preoccupation with bondage, including handcuffs, ropes and chains.

Men who find difficulty performing along more conventional sexual lines (that is, without well-defined prearrangements) begin to think of themselves as jaded, which is to say, impotent. Some turn to S&M, believing what we would call specious propaganda that sadomasochism is a form of sexuality suitable for those who have exhausted more conventional sex behavior. Some sadists and masochists are still capable of performing along more conventional lines, but their performances are usually structured, at least in their own minds, and take place with strangers. Long-term S&M relationships can't survive without distinct coordination and allocation of observances and functions.

We would advance the following theory as part of an explanation of the growing prevalence of sadomasochism:

It is generally agreed that the sexual revolution, with its undue emphasis on proper positioning and performance, has made many men highly uncomfortable (both in straight and gay society). Hyper self-consciousness helps to create impotence. Men try to rid themselves of this unwanted awareness, to forget themselves in the midst of sexual passion and simply to *enjoy*, but the structured, categorizing, logic-oriented and sequential nature of Western minds makes such forgetting a difficult task. Such men are faced with the feeling that they are incapable of mental and physical disassociation in the midst of the sex act, always being *aware* of precisely what they're doing and how they're positioning their limbs or any part of the body. Society's negative and puritanical emphasis on such positions heighten the predicament.

It is no coincidence, therefore, that many in the S&M crowd are religiously oriented and are known to attend churches. The dogma of atonement, involving as it does *agony* as payment for "sins," is not foreign to them. Nor is it a coincidence that the element of punishment for the performance of sexual acts (and as a corollary to their enjoyment) is paramount in sadomasochistic ritual.

The sadomasochistic approach to sexuality differs in its values from our own. We would emphasize tenderness and pleasure—in a sense we are anti-technological, preferring the human body. Sadomasochism emphasizes control and power and, in its use of artifacts, is highly technological.

79

TEA AND SYMPATHY

Hello, Young Lovers!

As I started reading your article on the subject of lesbianism, I ran into the name of the well-known film actress, Deborah Kerr, which made me read on faster for more mention of her. I soon found that you were not talking about Deborah Kerr herself, but of someone who is her look-alike. I relaxed quickly! You had mentioned that she (the look-alike) was a blonde university official. Anyway, since I am the president of the *only* Deborah Kerr fan club around—her huge portrait is staring down on me at this moment as I look up—I was wondering how much this woman looked like Deborah Kerr. Does she also have blueish-green eyes or wouldn't you know about that. Is there a photograph of this look-alike lady which could be parted with? I would keep it in great secrecy in my files.

> Very concernedly yours,
> Erhard U.
> Brooklyn, New York

Dear Erhard,

We're sorry but the lesbian in question is a bit finicky about sending her photo to a strange man's ''secret'' file.

Don't feel too badly though. We took another look at her and decided she didn't look like Deborah Kerr after all. She looks more like Gloria Grahame.

•

FROM BODY BEAUTIFUL

Gentleman,
I hear tell in the newspaper I read that some of your writers are gay. If they are, I would be very interested in hearing from them. Especially Lige and Jack.

I am 19 years of age, 6'2'' tall, weigh 174 lbs. and am well endowed. I have been told by quite a few that I have a beautiful body.

I would be very interested in getting a reply.

> Thank you,
> Don M.
> Birmingham, Alabama

Dear Don,
How nice for you that you are well endowed. With brains, we presume. With charm. With great sensitivity and kindness and most hopefully, with the ability to give, give, give!

•

RINGS ON YOUR
FINGERS AND . . .

Dear Lige and Jack:
Come on guys, let us in on the secret. What is a cock ring and where do you buy one (or two)? We are way out here in the boonies where they still use rubbers.

> Love & Peace & good vibes,
> Fred H.
> Rolling Meadows, Illinois

Dear Fred,

Cock rings are metal contrivances which fit over one's testicles. They are tight fitting and, we think, exceedingly uncomfortable. Those who use them swear that they help maintain a state of physical sexual excitation even when interest is flagging. They seem to be most popular among the leather and S&M crowds.

If you wish to buy one, check with the proprietor of your local erotic bookstore, or wait until you go to a large city where one of the stores which sell sex items can offer you your pick of sizes. Perhaps, even, they may provide a backroom where you can try them on for size.

For our money, they're not worth it. Guess we're afraid of breaking teeth on cold metal rings. Flesh seems a more intriguing fetish. Wearing a cock ring must be similar to wearing a splint.

•

EAT A REPUBLICAN FOR LUNCH

Dear Lige and Jack:

You're constantly making nasty cracks and slurs against President Nixon and the Republican party.

You should be reminded that there are thousands of nice gay folks who live in the suburbs of Long Island, Westchester and New Jersey who are Republicans and who respect our President.

Your editorial attitude is that all gay guys live in the Democratic ghettos of New York City. Why don't you wake up?

> Yours,
> Jim R.
> Sayville, L.I., New York

82

Dear Jim,
We'll start courting Republican politicians when they start playing knees with us! The Democrats have already started wooing us and we just love it!

•

PISTOL-PACKING LOVER

Dear Lige and Jack,
I've just finished reading your article, "Are You a Jealous Lover?" and was amazed at your reasoning about jealousy.

You're condoning lovers who seek extracurricular activity in an attempt to add excitement to their lives, so they can share it with one another. BALLS! If you can't have all your excitement and passion together you shouldn't be lovers. My interpretation of lovers? Two people in love.

I met my one and only (the good Lord willing) lover when I was a freshman in college. At the time he was an assistant professor and twelve years my senior. That was eleven years ago come September. Since that time I have never—and he assures me he has never—bedded with another. Desire, urge, curiosity, yes, but actuality, never.

Does it bother me when I see someone undressing him with their eyes or brushing close for a fleeting feel? You bet your sweet ass it does, and it works both ways (no pun intended).

The only ugly outburst of jealousy that ever threatened our relationship occurred while we were on a tour of Europe in 1963. Our guide, a greasy-looking foreigner, made it obvious that he was pursuing my lover. Your article implies I should have stood in the wings, watched the performance and been grateful that my lover was attractive to someone else. Over my dead body, darling. Had a cameraman been available I would have been a contender for the Oscar that year. (Who did win for '63?)

Your article on jealousy leads one to believe that your lover comes home after screwing some fairy and you greet him with open arms and are pleased that others find him sexually attractive. BULLSHIT! I hope that will never be my experience because if my lover did such a thing and I found out (definite proof, of course) I would wait until he was sleeping and then put a bullet in his brain. Your article implies that I would be a moron or a jerk for doing such a thing. But I justify being what I am by being in love with one guy. This theory puts me one step above a common cocksucker.

If you want sexual freedom, don't take a lover. But if you want a lover, have a whole one, not one you're sharing with half the town.

Moron/Jerk
Boston, Massachusetts

Dear Moron/Jerk,
Paranoid blindness kept you from grasping the essentials in our article on jealousy.

We said that it's often good to mix, sexually or otherwise, with many different people. Adventuresome lovers have more to share whenever they return to each other. Real sexual freedom, based on affectionate motives, is seldom used to excess.

It's good for any relationship to allow itself space. With space comes perspective, so each partner can better see and appreciate the other, as we can see a mountain's beauty more clearly from a distance than if we remain on top of it.

Men who are really secure in their love for each other don't fret away their good time in jealous snits.

What a capitalist/Calvinist you must be in bed, demanding the precise return of your investments!

Please don't cast disparaging remarks at "cocksuckers." Good cocksuckers are rare.

Really, Moron/Jerk, you seem more concerned with the dull preservation of your ego's little habit patterns than with giving your lover a buoyant, affirmative freedom that says, "I love you and I trust that you will always find me warm, exciting company."

That you would consider putting a bullet through your lover's brain, proof or no proof, when he's asleep, shows not only that you are unable to face him honestly and directly but that you love only yourself. Such a fantasy takes your jealousy out of mundane spheres to the border of lunacy, where you, dear "loving" soul, could easily graduate from being an uptight nerd to a sorry murderer. You need help.

• • •

JEALOUSY

Jealousy has its origins in insecurity and more often than not is uncalled for. The more insecure one feels, the greater will be one's jealous reactions. Self-esteem is the most potent weapon with which we can fight our own jealousy. Also, it is wise to remember that a brief flirtation, an obvious compliment to another, a night out, or a sexual encounter on the part of one's lover is hardly ever a reasonable cause for insecurity. The effects of such occasions most often become painfully swollen because they are taken so seriously. Thus one's jealousies and insecurities usually do more damage to a relationship than any event on which they're based.

Often lovers hold each other too tightly and, as in dancing, when they do so they're clumsy.

Those who practice the opposite extreme, wandering too far from each other in the name of freedom, also risk injury to their relationship. The ideal of sexual liberty is frequently abused. Couples would be wise to reassure one another that each is deeply loved before seeking too much independence either with others or with hobbies and work.

Nowadays it's fashionable for gay men to agree on sexual freedom *at the start* of their relationship and in many cases love affairs of this type thrive. It depends on the men involved. Obvious dangers exist for those who spend too much time outside the union, particularly if such outside "freedom" involves a rapid succession of sexual encounters with strangers. Under a banner of promiscuity, one or both men may find it difficult to acquire a sense of relationship-in-depth, in which a bond of mutual commitment is necessary.

COWBOY LAND

Dear Sirs,
I am a gay person in a big cowtown. I have just finished reading

The Gay Crusaders which contains a chapter about you. Before reading the book, I knew that there were other gay people, but I hadn't realized that there were any brave enough to stand up for all of us.

We have a lot of gay people in Omaha, but they are afraid to come out of their closets. About two years ago, when I came out, we used to have trouble at the bar we went to almost every night. It's getting a little better.

Do you know a lot of gay people? If so, what sort of lives do they lead? I would like some information. Keep on. May God bless you and keep you safe.

> Sincerely,
> Gary C.
> Omaha, Nebraska

Dear Gary,

Cowboys call it "messing around," you know, and they usually don't do it in the city. But out on the range, it's a different story.

Yes, even in the big cowtowns, things are a bit better than they were a few years ago, but still you may not see as many relaxed, self-assured gay people who truly are out of their closets.

What sort of people do we know? What kind of lives do they lead? We've met many happy and mature gay people from every walk of life. We've also met some real nut jobs.

•

FOUR SERIOUS PROBLEMS

Dear Lige and Jack,

I would like to thank you for answering my last letter so soon. I know you must receive many letters every day and considering this, I think you answered my letter rather promptly.

But now I am faced with another problem. I have a lover who has a few problems which create difficulties in our relationship. First, I should say that I'm only seventeen, living at home in Brooklyn with my parents, and my lover lives in Manhattan.

My lover's problems are:

1. He is a very heavy drinker.

2. He is a constant liar.

3. He is out of work and throws his unemployment check away.

4. He has a crazy idea that I should stop calling all my friends and ex-lovers I knew before I met him.

Now what I want to know is should I put up with this or should I forget it and find someone new?

Why I wrote *you* was because you were so helpful with my last problem.

> Sincerely,
> Bernard B.
> Brooklyn, New York

Dear Bernard,

It would seem that your lover is the "dreamboat" everybody's looking for!

Tell him to shape up or you'll ship out. It's for his own good, not only yours.

As for not calling your old friends and lovers, what kind of clinging vine is this lover of yours? Never allow *anyone* to start choosing your friends for you. That's *your* business. Remember: We're influenced by the kind of company we keep, even if we don't realize it at the time. Perhaps you need healthier friends.

•

SPIC 'N' SPAN

Dear Lige and Jack,

Congratulations to you for the excellent work you are doing for the gay community at large. This you are accomplishing by general news, education and information concerning entertainment.

I have only one complaint: this has to do with your (I feel) unnecessary use of vulgar language. I feel this hurts the image of the average homosexual. In fact the only reason I have not shown your newspaper to certain "straight" persons is that I would be embarrassed by the dirty language. I have no objection to the use of any kind of language if it is necessary to adequately put across a point or meaning.

I am not so naive as not to realize that there is a very fine line dividing the vulgar from non-vulgar, and opinions surely vary. But except in rare necessary occasions I think the word "shit" is filthy and need not be used. Even your best writers seem to have such a limited vocabulary that they are unable to find a cleaner substitute word.

> Sincerely yours,
> J.H.W.
> Wilmington, Delaware

Dear J.H.W.,
A substitute word? Feces, perhaps? Or manure?

THE RETURN OF
SPIC 'N' SPAN

Dear Lige and Jack,
I am more than a little perturbed by your comment concerning

my criticism of the use of the word shit, *viz.*, "A substitute word? Feces, perhaps? Or manure?" Surely this is a flippant, irrelevant reply. My criticism has to do with the fact that the word shit is used in your columns for things other than shit! It is used to denote all kinds of disagreements, frustrations, etc. In short, it is a figure of speech. Therefore I still insist that any columnist who cannot make use of other words is extremely limited in his vocabulary and imagination.

J.H.W.
Wilmington, Delaware

Dear J.H.W.,
Please, sir, excuse our flippancy. We'll try to get our shit together.

•

"AM I TOO CAUTIOUS?"

Dear Lige and Jack,
I've been seeing a bright, fairly conservative man for eight months now. We really enjoy each other immensely and spend much of our week together. As a matter of fact I love him, I think. However, neither of us has ever brought up the subject. I'm not really sure how he feels about me. We're both professionals but this can be an asset to us both. Are we being too formal or just too cautious?

Peace and love,
Stanley M.
Peoria, Illinois

Dear Stanley,

A little caution never hurts unless it masks fear. Eight months is a bit long to be formal, especially if you're together much of each week. If your relationship is good, as you say, there's no reason to rush to definitions of just who you are to each other and precisely what it means. We do hope, however, that your "caution" and "formality" don't include chastity.

Declaring undying love, in words, isn't nearly as important as just loving, and showing that we do in our daily life.

Try calling him "cutie pie" or "honey-man" or "sweet 'ums." See what happens.

•

LOOKING FOR A WOMAN

Dear Fellows,

About a year ago I discovered that I much prefer to sleep with another woman than with a man. After a few months my husband discovered what was going on and before I knew what was happening we had flown to Nevada and gotten a divorce. Since I don't really have any particular place I would call home, I decided to stay here. My problem is how to go about finding other women who are lesbians as I am.

> Sincerely,
> Racine W.
> Reno, Nevada

Dear Racine,

Social idiocies have made it tough, unfortunately, for women to meet one another in comfortable settings. We've been to lots of women's bars in our day and a few have been OK, but regular bar patrons, no matter what their sex or persuasion, aren't usually the cream of the crop.

In larger cities there are now a great many more all-women's organizations and we understand that scads of gay women have engaged themselves in the feminist struggle. Also, check with your local gay lib group either in town or in a nearby college and they'll gladly steer you to a social spa or to a scheduled function where you can meet gay women.

•

FIRED

Dear Lige and Jack,
I am a homosexual and was dismissed from my first position last year. I went to Pan Am after completing college. It was my first job. I attended school in the summer in order to finish college in three years.

My parents and family knew that I was a homosexual when I came back from school. I never tried to hide this fact from my friends and others. I was told that my appearance and personality was desired for my position at Pan Am. They did not know I was gay nor did I act as such. I began to spend some time in the city where other homosexuals meet and discovered many employees from my company were there. These people were not only from the reservations and related departments, either. I made the mistake of letting others know of my way of life. When asked where I went for the weekend, I would tell them, even if it was known to be a place for gays. Some people think that Fire Island is exclusively for homosexuals and look upon all who go there as such.

I will admit I never dated any male or even female personnel from this company. I did have a party where I invited some employees, both gay and straight, and I attended parties with my lover (whom I've known since our college days). We were always accepted by these people and we respected each other's way of life.

One day I received an intra-company memo, not signed, from a "friend" telling me I was going to be dismissed within the week because they don't like to have homosexuals in the company. I was advised to deny I was a homosexual and fight them. Two days later I was told to leave the company. I did not fight them and after looking for a job for one day, I started to work for an advertising company in the city. They are more liberal regarding homosexuals, but to this day I keep it a secret from most of my fellow employees.

I feel that I am a good citizen. I have a high-paying job. I help out in community affairs and I should not be looked upon as abnormal.

My family, friends and lover all live a normal life. I have given my time during the elections and have helped the school system with my volunteer work. I am an asset to my community on Long Island and feel that I should be accepted whether gay or otherwise. Those whom I have worked with in the community don't know I am a homosexual. I know that if they did know, their attitude would change toward me.

Now, when I look back, I realize I was foolish not to fight for my rights.

> Roger
> Long Island, New York

Dear Roger,
Take heart. You're not the only one that Pan Am has dismissed. They also fired one of our friends, an international flight stewardess—not a lesbian—for *writing* about sex. Pan Am is simply retarded about sex. Its attitudes about sexual variation

93

are as current as its cattle-car carriers. Pan Am is the loser in your case, not you. You were on the up and up and the airline has cheated itself by firing an honest man. If it ever happens again, raise a stink! Most companies would prefer to keep an employee to having him picket with a ''homosexual picket sign'' outside. ''Queers'' marching at the front door are marvelous embarrassments to uptight employers.

•

THE PRISONER'S PLIGHT

Dear Jack and Lige,
The many recent prison uprisings have brought light to the abominable dehumanizing conditions which inmates are forced to endure. Any gay prisoner can attest to the excruciating mental and often physical anguish to which he/she is subjected above and beyond that of the rest of the prison population.

Often incarcerated for political reasons, the gay prisoner must increasingly receive the fruits of the liberation efforts of those of us who are not so bodily confined. It is his due.

It is time more of us established communications with our sisters and brothers in jails. They need us desperately. A first step is mere human contact. Gay prisoners frequently want to correspond with individuals by mail. They want to know what is happening in the community.

A brother in the Marion, Illinois, Penitentiary has been writing me. He may have to remain in solitary for a year. He wants to receive gay publications and so do many others like him.

It would be great if gay newspapers were to establish a fund whereby subscriptions for inmates would be subsidized by those of us who can afford it.

Let us destroy the isolation of gay prisoners from our community. They have a lot to offer us.

> Sincerely,
> Morty Manford
> New York City

Dear Morty,
Your concern is edifying. There are now several groups communicating with gay prisoners, many of which operate through the gay Metropolitan Community Churches and through some of the gay liberation organizations. Gay publications would indeed be wise to institute the kind of fund you recommend. George Bernard Shaw said: "As long as there is one man behind bars, we are all imprisoned."

● ● ●

BEHIND THE SCENES

While the so-called experts sit at conference tables debating the nature of sexual orientation, or listening to papers composed by psychiatric theorists, a young man is returning home somewhere carrying an undesirable discharge from the Armed Forces which will blight the remainder of his life.

While these same "authorities" are spending years doing "research" on atypical gay people who've felt the need to visit psychiatrists, somewhere a mother or a father has recoiled from their gay child, horrified and repulsed.

95

While clergymen, psychologists, professors and penologists study graphs and percentages, all over America, in offices both large and small, are millions of gay employees—capable and kind people who work conscientiously, spending years in the service of their firms. Many of these employees worry every day about loss of their livelihoods should some "superior" suspect that their sex life doesn't conform to his standards.

•

AFTER THE MARRIAGE, WHAT?

Greetings Lige and Jack,

I've been "out" less than a year—came through seventeen years of marriage, six kids and a divorce to the point of realization that I was trapped and miserable in the closet. Now I know who I am! And you know, I've had sex with four different married men during this past year who are as miserable as I was.

My lover and I have been talking about some kind of organization of gays for this section of the state. If you have any suggestions or referrals to make, we'd be most appreciative.

Thanks for being such great heads!

Jay D.
Detroit, Michigan

Dear Jay,

We do hope you can still be close to your wife and six kids too. Seventeen years is a long time to dangle your family in front of divorce before deciding to live the life that of late you've found so charming. Your levels of awareness have taken so long to change, in fact, that you should—in fairness—always be tolerant of those in your family who find it difficult to appreciate the beauty of your life.

There are gay lib organizations in your area—but if you want to start one with your own slant, check out the needs of your community. It might help if you were "out" a bit longer than a year, however, as experience and a wider knowledge makes for a better gay lib leader.

•

A MARRIED MAN

Dear Sirs,

This is a story you've probably heard many times. I've been married twenty-two years, have a good wife and lovely children who think the world of me, yet I'm gay, unknown to them or any members of my family. My parents are deceased.

I married because my brothers and sisters were always after me and made me feel so bad always saying, "Why don't you find a girl and get married, it's not right for you to stay single."

If the people in our town knew twenty years ago that I was gay, I would have been put away in a nut house or something similar.

Even though my family is close to me I'm very lonely, living in a world by myself. I need someone whom I can write or talk to. You must know someone.

Lonely,
Larry J.
Michigan

Dear Larry,
Get a post-office box and place a few pen-pal ads in the gay publications.

• • •

COMING OUT   PART II

Coming out should not mean a backward focus on one's homosexuality. It should mean a forward look to how one can put his desires to work to create a happier life. A better word for coming out might be *discovering*!

Once out a wise person bypasses homosexuality as being inconsequential. It assumes its place along with other aspects of his life. He realizes that because society has made such a fuss he's allowed the subject to claim so much of his own attention.

This step helps him appreciate that people, gay or straight, share problems having little to do with sexual orientation, often rooted in a contemptible social structure. Anti-homosexuality is seen as the outgrowth of a larger ailment: anti-sexuality.

Those who've ceased to occupy themselves with being in the "proper" sexual category, begin to think instead about the quality they can bring to their lives. They learn how to preserve good relationships, to make them more responsive to their needs and to protect them from the onslaughts of insidious social coercion.

Our immediate surroundings (such as needed space and comfort in our apartments and homes) count for a great deal, as do the wider environs where all must live and work.

The invisible enemy of happiness, social coercion, waits everywhere to ensnare emotions, whether gay or straight. Once our sensibilities have been freed from unimportant considerations they are still subjected to a host of impulses waiting in every "civilized" corner to harness them again.

Advertising is filled with such impulses. A sensitive man is subjected to a daily barrage wherever he turns. What is lamentable about this is not, as is commonly assumed, the poor quality of the products advertised. Nor is it the inane jingles and ditties used for promotion. The snare lies in the *values* which advertising covertly promotes.

Look at how it depicts relationships, for example. Homosexually inclined men and women should beware of such stereotypical displays, but heterosexual couples should resent them even more. Initially, some may laugh when angry feminists object to ads showing subserviant wives slaving at washing machines for "hubby." Thoughtful people soon realize that such exhibits *do* reinforce and maintain despicable social arrangements which cause untold misery in the homes of millions whose lives, if they broke out of antiquated moulds, might be infinitely happier.

Advertising promotes a preoccupation with fashions too; fashions which change rapidly enough so that capitalists realize a tidy profit each time a season goes by. This, in itself, wouldn't be nearly so bad were it not for the fact that advertising generally stresses the importance of the superficial: of using *outer garments* as a means of *creating an impression* on others and hence as the way to promote the wearer to happiness and success. This approach is ugly. An informed public would be wise to raise its objections.

Similar objections might be leveled at promotions of drugs such as aspirin, nicotine, tension relievers and alcohol. These substances encourage people to rely not on their own inner resources to maintain equilibrium but on outside propulsions. At every turn people are imperceptibly led away from themselves and toward exterior dependence.

Another malignancy is sentimentality, often regulated by such media as the lyrics of top-selling songs. The songs bombard us everywhere—in jukeboxes, on the radio, in cabarets and nightclubs. Too many of them promote banal ideas about love and romance, leaving their mark on people of all sexual orientations.

Sentiment is the refuge of those who cling to fond hopes by turning their attention toward yesterday. Advertising know-how takes advantage of such frailties and has cleverly turned absorption with the past, with re-remembering, into big business. A song's familiar refrain, like a saved memento, calls to us to *mummify* our emotional lives. There is something basic in people which responds to repetition. It lulls them by reversion to the familiar. Familiarity, no matter how comfortable it makes us feel, represents a danger. If coming out is to take on the aura of *discovery* we, as explorers, can't always expect to be comfortable. To flee habits and repetitiveness is to refresh our lives with a *now* quality.

How many gay lovers, or straight husbands and wives, are caught in routines and customs? How many are missing the spontaneity of untamed schedules and have allowed their relationships to degenerate into etiquette, stifling their natural sympathies?

Social coercion grips all too many lives because social institutions don't teach us to take control of *ourselves*, but on the contrary, to be controlled. The churches offer us our moral codes. The military teaches us to obey. Employers ask us to be highly circumspect. Relatives request that we keep "good" our family name. We are the beneficiaries of mental customs, inheriting ideas and opinions and depending *not on ourselves* but on those who supposedly know more than we do about the fitness of things.

To appear "with it" and "successful" according to patterns set by *Playboy* or *After Dark* (a closet case's dream), many who call themselves gay—but are, in fact, grim —spend a great deal of time futzing with fashion, allowing social norms to determine the arrangement or rearrangement of exteriors: their clothes, their apartments, and the like. Such people seek beauty, not within, which is in fact where it really comes from, but from trinkets they hang on themselves or on their walls.

They spend their time polishing externals under the illusion that they are doing something for themselves, when, in fact, they are really doing something for their wardrobes and their apartments. They are striving to give their lives a sense of order and purpose. They bypass tasks which might lead to self-improvement in a more direct way.

FROM SOUTH AFRICA

Dear Lige and Jack,
A friend of mine who has just returned from the States brought me the current issue of one of your publications. I thoroughly enjoyed reading it and was very envious at the freedom gays

enjoy in the U.S.A. compared to us in South Africa. I would like to subscribe but I doubt if it would be let into the country. Anything like that is scrupulously banned here; even magazines like *Playboy*!

Gays are persecuted here and we have to be very discreet although we do have the brazen ones who don't care a damn, but in the end they only make things harder for the others. Gay life here where I live is absolutely dead, but livelier in Durban and Johannesburg where there is quite a big movement. Several clubs there cater to gays, but these are an ordeal to go to as they are constantly raided by the police.

I am what you might call a "butch gay" over here. I am a keen Rugby (football) fan and also do a bit of surfing. I take out a girl for a front and have the occasional gay "fling." My parents don't know about me—like most parents here, they're very narrow-minded as far as gays are concerned.

I am twenty-one years old, six feet tall with brown hair and eyes. My interests are pop music, movies, reading and writing and interior decorating.

I would appreciate it very much if you could tell me how to get in touch with gays in the States wanting to correspond, in the twenty-one-to-thirty age group.

Yours sincerely,
M.C.
Republic of South Africa

Dear M.C.,
Thanks for the candid view of what's going on down under. What we know as "liberty" or "freedom" grows in different locales at various velocities. Let's hope both your country and

ours can learn more about respect for human rights and civil liberties.

Yes, we enjoy many freedoms here in the good ol' U.S.A., but one of our patriots once warned that liberty's price is constant vigilance.

Democracy everywhere must inevitably grant the right of citizens to form deep personal attachments irrespective of gender. An intense and loving comradeship between those of the same sex is integral with a fuller extension of democracy.

To get in touch with friends in the U.S.A., put a pen-pal ad in any of the gay publications your friend gave you.

●

SEX BEHIND THE
IRON CURTAIN

Dear Jack and Lige,
My reason for writing is to get some information or advice. I'm going to be visiting the Soviet Union. I have been told to abstain from all forms of sex for the two-week trip. It is rumored that all hotel rooms are bugged, thereby making any activity highly dangerous.

Gratefully yours,
Leonard W.
Fort Worth, Texas

Dear Leonard,
Playing peek-a-boo behind the iron curtain is risky. Puritanical ethics survive and penetrate Soviet society so thoroughly that there are no gay bars in the entire nation. A gathering of

homosexually inclined people or a gay lib group would be unthinkable in Moscow.

The Cuban government, another "people's" regime, isolates known gay people in concentration camps.

Latin American right-wing dictatorships and juntas aren't very inspiring either. The *macho* male will be slow to go south of the border.

Gay Americans can appreciate the freedoms we enjoy and many are realizing it's wise to work hard so they won't be stripped from us.

Gay life in the United States swings more vibrantly and openly than in any other country. Even the Scandinavian countries, with their legal freedoms, can't match the goings-on in certain cities in the land of Uncle Sam.

●

NEIGHBORS TO THE NORTH

Dear Sirs,

After reading some of America's gay publications I've been surprised to see that the American public does know something of the laws we have in this country, Canada. Many Americans whom I have had the pleasure to meet and talk to are surprised about Canada's stand on matters concerning sex. As they point out, we do have strong censorship of movies and foreign publications coming into this country, but we are not as conservative in thinking as many American states when it comes down to homosexuality, which has been legalized in this country. We also do not have a law which forbids a homosexual to join the Armed Forces. We may not be able to read or see pornography in the movies or magazines, but at least our government, and the

Royal Canadian Mounted Police, do stay out of the nation's bedrooms.

> Thank you,
> B.N.
> Alberta, Canada

Dear B.N.,
Your country is new and exciting! Too bad its immigration laws still discriminate against gays.

We visited Toronto in 1973 as guest speakers for Gay Pride Week, sponsored by the Community Homophile Association of Toronto. We found that city to be blessed with one of the sanest police forces, as well as one of the most delightful gay communities in North America.

● ● ●

DEMOCRATIC SAFEGUARDS

Homosexual feelings are of great value in every society. They cause surprise—which is both healthy and necessary—to those who assume that human feelings can be expressed in only one mold.

Homosexuality is a needed form of heresy everywhere, one which nature weaves both subtly and openly into the fabric of every culture. It presents all conformists with an unsettling dilemma if they have not yet reached that stage of democratic discernment which allows for personal/private variations.

The person who claims the right to live his sex life free from the meddling of neighbors, churches, employers and

105

the State, lends new dimensions to the concept of *primacy of the individual*.

He requests the right to be soverign of his own body, thoughts and emotions, as should every man in a truly free society.

He asks for new amplitudes in freedom of the press: the right to celebrate the joy of his own perspective.

He protests the ever-watchful eye of Big Brother who gathers data on the sex lives of citizens and uses *differences* in sex orientation to eliminate political and cultural opposition. (Witness such snooping by the U.S. Government, the Cuban Government and other regimes, both capitalist and socialist.)

His very presence is a rebuke to the anti-democratic tendency to dismiss a man and to hound him through the remainder of his life because of his private thoughts and passions.

THE BOSS

Dear Jack and Lige,

I've been working for three months as a computer programmer for a respectable firm. Today my boss and I were alone in his office and he told me he'd been wanting to ''get to know me better.'' Honest, I didn't even know he was gay, he's married

106

with two children. He wants me to get together with him next week while his wife is out of town on business. He's a great boss, a good person to work for but I don't have any desire to do anything further with him. I'm just afraid he's going to get steadily more aggressive and I do need the job.

Sincerely,
Lynn H.
Memphis, Tennessee

Dear Lynn,
There are three ways to handle a boss like yours. There's the good straightforward lie: tell him you're hung up on another person and that it's reciprocal. Say you're the faithful type, but you'd be glad to introduce him to your best friend, Arnold Auchincloss, who's looking for love, something he's never had.

The second method is insidiously deceptive: create a less sexy you right in front of his eyes. Swish a little. Take off an afternoon to see the doctor about a possible hemorrhoidectomy. Rap casually, expressing hope that your syph is a thing of the past, adding that the last blood tests you took contradicted each other. Drool.

The final way, of course, is to say you'd be glad to get together with him and his wife anytime he invites you over, providing your lover can stand your absence. Or tell him, simply, that you could never cheat on *his* wife, adding sweetly that if he doesn't protect his own immortal soul from sin, that you, his faithful servant must act as his conscience. Tell him he'll thank you someday.

•

"PUT A GALLON IN
ME ALLEN!"

Dear Lige and Jack,
I hope you can help settle an argument my lover and I are having.

He doesn't go out on me—that much I know. But there's one thing he does do that I think is very thoughtless and unkind.

Every time we stop for gas he gets out of the car and flirts with the station attendants. Some of them don't know he's flirting, but a few do. It's embarrassing. Anyway, I know, and that's what counts.

He says it's just harmless fun, but it's no fun for me. What do you think I should do? Or do you think I should just do nothing?

Frank P.
Ardmore, Pennsylvania

Dear Frank,
Get rid of the car and take the bus!

•

MY FRIEND MIGHT
HATE ME

Dear Jack and Lige,
Remember that special friend you shared your childhood with, the one that would almost give his life for you but if he found out you were gay he'd probably hate you? I do. But I love my friend for his being himself and I accept his ignorance. If he finds out that I'm gay, that's life. Until that moment, I will secretly try to change his attitudes. If it doesn't work only God can help him.

What would be the easiest way of letting him know his purview is limited?

> Friend in need,
> Ralph D.
> Las Vegas, Nevada

Dear Ralph,

Are you really sure your friend would "hate" you? After all these years? Are your shared experiences so insignificant to him? Must you—as his friend—condone the fact that he's tightassed? Must real friends try to change one another's sexual prejudices so secretly, failing to be open and honest?

God, dear slowpoke, works much faster through busy hands. How can you let your friend know that his purview is limited? Stage a candlelight supper—just you and him—Rachmaninoff on the Victrola and a gourmet's delights to tempt his palate. Then, when the candles flicker convulsively and the music reaches its peak, grasp him suddenly, plant a kiss squarely on his oral cavity, stick your finger up his ass and whisper sweet nothings in his ear. Say, "Don't be surprised, my love, *this is your destiny!*"

● ● ●

HYPOCRITES

How is it possible to revere the Virgin Mary but to give and receive so blessedly in the dunes at Fire Island? How can a young man who insists his lover be "true" frolic in a Turkish bath while away on a business trip? Why does a gay actor, who feels in private that he's "liberated," insist on taking a female escort he hardly knows to a cast party?

Would it be impudent to suggest that the man who might do one of these things would also be likely to do the others, too?

BLONDS OR BRUNETS?

Dear Lige and Jack,
I only like blonds and can't even stand being in the same room with Latins. My roommate (a blond) only likes Puerto Ricans and hates blonds. Neither of us can bring a trick home now without arguments. What the hell can I do?

> Need help,
> F.P.
> Philadelphia, Pennsylvania

Dear F.P.,
MOVE!

•

SEX CULTISM

Dear Lige and Jack,
I was considerably satisfied to read in your "Editors Speak" column that you would "like to see the words 'homosexual' and

'heterosexual' fade away.'' Good. But this can only happen when homosexuals stop trying to gain acceptance for themselves as homosexuals or gays rather than as individual human beings.

Too many of our younger homosexuals who consider themselves liberated are still riddled with guilt. In servile self-defense they establish their own churches, their own gathering places, their own special way of life (or life-style as it is now called) and their own homosexual culture. They are trying to make a cult out of a sex act.

Intelligent heterosexuals are fast breaking out of their centuries-old, self-imposed sexual straitjackets. We should not allow the homosexual to fall into that kind of bondage. What we need most is a sense of personal worth and independence. There is no special place in this world for homosexuals!

> Cordially,
> Don S.
> Los Angeles, California

Dear Don,
Your letter reflects the true spirit of liberation. It's for everyone, not just so-called homosexuals. Strong identification with any group—either a sexual majority or a sexual minority—doesn't often allow a person to expand comfortably beyond the culturally prescribed borders of his or her group.

•

DON'T LET LIFE PASS YOU BY!

Dear Lige and Jack,
I am always angered and somewhat bewildered when I hear

111

various doctors, law-enforcement officials and politicians refer to us with their "sickness-immoral-social problem" phraseology. But I am more angered and bewildered, and even saddened, when I read letters from certain gay folks giving us a view of their "gay" life, which for many is anything but "gay" and hardly a "life" at all.

Are these people so wrapped up in self-pity and fear to realize that whether a person is hetero or homo he has a choice: To make the best he possibly can of his life, or let it all pass by? It's a sobering thought when you realize we have only one chance. Just one short chance. How can anyone consider throwing that chance away?

It is difficult to comprehend how we can expect understanding, respect or even a passive "live and let live" attitude from heterosexuals if so many of us show such a despairing attitude toward homosexuality by going through a self-punishing type of existence. The plea "There's no one else in the world like me. . . . I'd like to know other gay people, but I'm too shy . . ." is nothing but a cop out. Each one of us has been afraid at some time. And most of us have neither the need nor desire to tell everyone that we're gay. Everyone does not have to know. But to be afraid of yourself and to be afraid of life is as destructive as those who would put us in jails or mental institutions for being what we are!

There have been millions of gay people in this world, and millions more will follow. But each of us is one—an individual—and our life is ultimately what we decide to make it. A city council may give us the "right" to buy a Central Park co-op without bias. But if all that is being bought is "loneliness with a view," all the laws in the world won't be worth a damn.

> Please sign me:
> Bill S.
> New York City

Dear Bill,

Bravo! You've found that liberation involves a significant kind of personal development. More and more people are seeing things your way. Don't let others make you too angry. Anger clouds good judgment. Instead, look closely at the new generation. The old guilt feelings are fading fast.

At the turn of the century one of the Western world's first gay liberationists, Edward Carpenter, said that "a kind of love that is tabooed, despised, talked about in washrooms and relegated to holes and corners, can hardly be expected to show its best side to the world."

We've been fortunate enough in recent years to meet men and women regularly who are showing that their love for others *can* show its best side to the world.

•

GOD IS ALIVE IN
A CAPSULE

Hello Folks,

I have some comments to make about "drugs." To me, grass and hash are pleasant improvements upon alcohol. They make the music more affecting and the colors brighter for the moment, but they leave my psyche untouched. LSD doesn't.

I, too, know people who should have stayed away from acid. The guys who drop it every week seem to me to be in deep trouble. Neither methedrine nor strychnine strikes me as being the ideal dietary supplement. And a bad trip is no fun at all.

I had spent a long time and a lot of energy building a great big thick wall between me and the rest of the world. Finally I began to realize that my life had become empty and sterile; I was the helpless prisoner of my wall. By then it was too late for me to change; habit had solidified. I thought wistfully about tearing

113

down my wall, but I knew that I never would; I didn't know how to begin, and besides, I was afraid. Known loneliness was safer than possible rejection. I know it sounds stupid but it happens to a lot of people.

Then someone turned me on to acid. My values changed. I decided that I had a right to be happy. I learned that I had something to offer others, and they had something to offer me. Affection, care, a smile, love? I'm not sure yet.

I am beginning to learn that the world around me is filled with beauty. All I have to do is look to enjoy it. I have a long, long road to travel, but because of my infrequent trips, I have made a start, and I am a happier man. Don't think I would have done it alone.

As you say, LSD is tricky and potentially dangerous stuff, and I guess there's no way to predict its effect upon any single individual. But I am one person whose "dismal approach toward living" has been improved considerably through its use. That's the other side of the coin.

Yours truly,
Hank K.
Phoenix, N.M.

Dear Hank,
Your story isn't atypical. Clinical research is still being done on LSD and some psychotherapists are using it in therapy. Its value under such circumstances has been greatly underrated, particularly since the late Sixties when Flower Power faded into the noisy confusion that allowed the unnecessary imprisonment of Dr. Timothy Leary.

But LSD can be very much abused too, and should therefore

114

be used in well-controlled situations. For many it has cleared away mental cobwebs and made life a clearer and less complicated experience.

Our only objection to drugs of any kind is that they are a variety of technology. There is nothing wrong with technology, per se, except that (as in the case with the automobile) it often dazzles us so that we rely on it to extremes. The average American, for example, spends 1,500 hours a year driving his car and earning money to store it, and pay for highway taxes. Ivan Illich, author of *Tools for Conviviality*, writes that "the advantages of absolute precedence of people over vehicles are so obvious that they have become invisible."

In a like manner, Americans have come to rely on drugs of many types instead of realizing that self-care has advantages, and that drugs should not take precedence over man's innate abilities to clear away his own cobwebs.

Given our countrymen's tendency to rely on technology —drugs become, more often than we like to think, psychologically indispensable. We've seen people who can't get it on without taking acid, poppers, mescaline, or ups and downs. It's sad.

Drugs interfere with the body's natural rhythms. If one wishes to get in touch with those rhythms—depending, as all self-regulating people would, on the *self* for the joy and magic of living—drugs may be seen as a furtive crutch.

A final word: a regular acid head waltzes on the edge of mistaking a day's limited perceptions—during a trip—for an absolutely clear view of whatever happens to be going on. This is not to say that this might not happen to non-drug users as well. But acid *does* provide a host of distinct impressions. Psychedelics have one undisputed effect: they make users impatient with structure, not only in the environment but in the minds (as structure is perceived) of one's closest friends and associates. While impatience with structure can be a good thing on the social level, it can be a bad thing for personal relationships. And, as we've said, a day's limited perception isn't the whole truth.

•

BIG MAN ON CAMPUS

Dear Jack and Lige,

In my fraternity house at school one of the brothers is constantly boasting of his hetero conquests. However, both of us know that he is gayer than a goose. (I've slept with him.) He refuses to join the campus homophile union and will not go to the bars. We are going to be roommates next year. Would it be advisable for me to be forward and ask him to liberate himself, or should I suffer by listening to his "fairy tales?"

Fondly,
B.C.
Pittsburgh, Pennsylvania

Dear B.C.,

Remember that each person has to live his own life, even if we feel it would be better to live differently. Don't try to pull him out of the closet by force. The best way is by example. When he sees your own enjoyment of gay life without hiding, he may begin to get the point. A few words to him would be OK, but do it gently. Let him know how refreshing it is to live openly with one's feelings. You could also point out that his boasting indicates he's hung up on the old "male conquering" attitude toward women. His problem is his fear of being out of step. Kindly help him to find his own rhythms, and to disregard those

116

of our dissolving, changing society, so that he may grow up and learn to enjoy *himself*.

●

OUTLAW LOVERS' LANE?

Dear Guys,

Re: Your stand on police harrassment of the Baths, Bravo!

But let's make it a knock-out punch! If the fuzz are on a "morals" "decency" kick, let us expose the straight hangouts and lovers' lanes.

Let the gay community direct the men in blue to the lovers' lanes of New York, where, in parked cars, the heterosexuals commit the same "criminal" acts we gay people are charged with when we carry on.

Under the Verrazano Bridge, along Ft. Hamilton Bay Bridge and Prospect Park are places notorious for straight parked-car sodomy and fellatio.

Yet these places are never raided. Why can't we have our docks and bath scenes if the straights can have theirs?

Remember . . . it's illegal for them too!

Thanks for listening.

> Tony,
> New York City

Dear Tony,

We've got no enmity for "straight" lovers. If they can sodomize and fellatiate, good for them. Let's work to make the fuzz let *everyone* alone!

●

MY WIFE AND I

Dear Lige and Jack,
Although straight, my wife and I are enthusiastic fans of yours.
Many straight people are afraid of the gay world. We think that
attitude is ridiculous. We think gays are great!

> Love,
> Dave and Liz
> New York City

Dear Dave and Liz,
Some gays are great and some aren't, but anyway it's encourag-
ing when folks like yourselves try to act as bridges between
spheres. There is no "straight" world or "gay" world in an
ideal sense: there is only *one* world—and in it, everybody is
loving.

●

G.I. JERK OFF

Dear Lige and Jack,
A friend of mine has been sending me occasional articles by the
two of you. I'm just finishing my tour of duty in Vietnam and
can't wait to get back home to the States and to New York. I
wish I could relate some "exotic" adventures of Vietnam to
you but no such luck. The most exciting thing that has happened
was when I jerked off three times the other night while on guard
duty! Oh well!

I think everyone over here has entered a closet and locked the door and thrown away the key. It's really difficult to find any action here.

Wishing,
E.A.
Vietnam

Dear E.A.,
Millions of fine young American men are anxiously awaiting your return. The revelation that American soldiers are jerking off on guard duty is quite "exotic," whether you realize it or not. It's too bad more young men aren't jerking off instead of doing so much "guarding." Dig this vision: thousands of soldiers moving—naked—in the steaming jungles, carrying —not guns—but their own genitals, and getting closer to one another in the dark. A saner behavior pattern by far than any war.

•

TIGHTASSED
TROUBLES

Dear Gentlemen,
My question is of a personal nature and I don't know if it is of general interest to the gay public, but it means a lot to me. I've had a lover for over a year. I love him very much and know he feels the same about me.

My problem is that when my lover and I are engaged in sexual activity I am unable to successfully enact the passive role. The reason for this is that I have never learned to relax properly. During each act of sex when I am on the receiving end I freeze up with the slightest bit of pain. This bothers me because I know that our relationship would benefit if my lover could successfully enter me. I've heard that there are products on the open market which allow your anal muscles to relax. If this is so please tell me how I can buy them, or tell me what you think I should do.

Sincerely yours,
Robert L.
New Mexico

Dear Robert,
Relaxation is the child of attitude, not of products on the open market. First, being fucked doesn't mean that you're into a role or that you're what society calls "passive." Any athlete must know how to step forward as well as he can step back. With some folks it takes a while. Others find that they just can't handle it, but this doesn't mean that we should think less of them for it.

Your pain is caused by anticipation which results in a tightening of your muscles, particularly your anal muscles. You brace yourself rigidly because you fear pain and your pains are caused when you brace yourself rigidly. Don't brace. Allow your body to fall forward. Otherwise you're caught in a vicious circle. The only other place where you may experience a similar tightening is in the dentist's chair.

Opening yourself requires resigning yourself trustfully into another's hands. The self-assurance shown by another can help in such a case. But don't let anyone lay a trip on you or your lover that says having difficulty being fucked means that you don't trust him or that he lacks self-assurance. Such heavy condemnations are not at all fair in this imperfectly advanced age of sexual discovery.

120

You are simply having a tough time learning to receive, to accept, to experience passively.

To learn this lesson, try to see yourself as a person who is receiving the experience of touch rather than as the one who touches. Instead of pursuing, allow yourself to be pursued. Enjoy watching yourself from a new dimension when, instead of feeling your lover, he feels you. Don't anticipate. Let him feel of you, turning you gently as he leads. Perhaps it might help to erase your fearfulness if you first allow him to manipulate you with his fingers. Guide him into you gently. A lubricant will help.

He should understand, of course, that it's important he move slowly, particularly if he too is not sexually experienced. Bring his mouth close to yours and breathe long warm breaths into him, again, slowly. If you sense his eagerness and his excitement, revel in it. It's for you!

Before any of this happens, however, you must accustom yourself to your anal tract. One reason you may "freeze up" as you say, is that you're not familiar enough with your own anal region. Don't forget that your ass, like many other parts of your body, is a natural erotic zone. People who say that asses are only for shitting are just as stupid as those who insist that peckers are only for pissing. Your ass is just as likely an erotic zone as is your mouth. It is open to sensual stimulation. Finally, caring for it is every bit as important as is caring for your mouth. You can't have one, you know, without the other.

•

WHAT A THRILL!

Dear Lige and Jack,
I have a problem. I am thirty-one years old and gay and would like to have anal intercourse, even though I'm quite butch. The

121

trouble is that I'm too nervous and it hurts too much. The only time it happened was a number of years ago when I didn't expect it . . . what a thrill! Any suggestions?

Love and peace,
Israel F.
Staten Island, New York

Dear Israel,
Yes—stop gritting your teeth, and wear a blindfold when you hop in the sack so you won't know what's going on. If it was once an unexpected thrill, maybe other things will happen to you too—as long as you don't anticipate—who knows—maybe your future holds a whole string of delights.

● ● ●

SEX PROBLEMS

Love affairs can't be based on sex alone. When a couple uses sex as a measuring stick for their success, making a point of it may be the very cause of their union's dissolution. Sexual attraction grows out of a spontaneous lifestyle free of rigid habit patterns. When it becomes a focus of critical attention, anxiety, selfconsciousness, pride and speculation rob it of its essential core: playfulness.

Society is rife with fraudulent ideals about sexual competence. These ideals cause men to worry about maintaining high sexual performance standards. Many men have become so nervous about performance that they're always worrying about whether or not they're touching properly, whether they're "good" and the like.

122

Society's ideals about what constitutes ability in this area have been produced by overzealous propagandists of the so-called sexual revolution. Those who have established such ideals (and we speak from personal contact with them in media), are seldom capable of meeting the high standards they've set themselves. What such people have failed to realize is that each person's levels of dexterity differ. Those who pass critical judgments, and make others feel less than sexually competent, are failing to do what constitutes the most loving sexual act of all: gently reaching for another and through touch making him feel *whole*. Such a critic also shows that he has failed to appreciate the variety of unique human dexterities and capabilities.

Concepts of sexual prowess hamper the ability of many men to relax and enjoy touching each other. They show concern with the size of their genitals, with the socially prescribed "need" for orgasm, with maintaining a constant erection and a brute "piston power" that allows them to "go for hours."

There is a different approach to sex that lacks these heavy compulsions. A man need not be so dominant in every respect at every moment during the sexual act. The difference in psychological attitude required for such situating is at the polar extreme from that which most men, in their everyday consciousness, adopt. Walt Whitman reveled in the passive state of being, and his poems are filled with lines such as:

I will go to the bank and become undisguised and naked.
I am mad for it to be in contact with me.

or when addressing the sea, he sings:

I believe you refuse to go back without feeling of me . . .
Hurry me out of the sight of land,
Cushion me soft, rock me in billowy drowse,
Dash me with amorous wet, I can repay you. . . .
I am intregal with you, I too am of one phase and of all phases
Partaker of influx and eflux I. . . .

The genius of Whitman's perception of self lay in the fact that he saw himself not as exclusively active or exclusively passive, but as a "partaker" of that which came to him and that which emanated from him: of "influx and eflux." He knew that men must learn what he called "the profound lesson of reception." This stance is a healthy one, not only for homosexuals but for all men who need desperately to allow openings in themselves for vital, active ingress. To be perpetually active is to tire oneself and to cause a needless state of anxiety.

From such a vantage point, "piston power" and the "need" for a constant erection would give way to a new order, finding sensual arousal in activities that don't require brute power. Fondling, rolling, fingering, touching, rubbing, stroking, sucking, kissing, licking, breathing, tickling and a host of other aimless pursuits would bring men to new levels of excitation and might better create a tendency to sexual procrastination, something which will be much needed as mankind finds itself with more and more leisure time.

• • •

VD DOUCHE?

Gentlemen,
My question to you is, are there any disinfectants on the market to protect one anally against VD? I have been told that a douche with strong solutions can be poisonous. Is this true? What would you suggest?

                    Yours truly,
                    L.E.
                    Little Rock, Arkansas

Dear L.E.,
We'd suggest an anal smear and a blood test every three months. Strong solutions can be hazardous and since the Federal Drug Administration is so lax about truly physically harmful substances, from shampoos to anal douches, blood tests and smears are still tops! If possible find a sane doctor in your town through friends, a gay organization, or the bartender at one of your local gay bars.

● ● ●

VENEREAL DISEASE

V.D., known as the gift that keeps on giving, is more commonly referred to as syph and/or clap.

Anyone who's had even moderate sexual experience should get a blood test for syphilis at least four times yearly. There's absolutely nothing to be ashamed of in such proceedings. In fact, the opposite is true. Those who don't get blood tests should feel ashamed and, in fact, dirty. It's like brushing one's teeth, keeping clean, and this new ethic, making sure that one has clean blood, must be established in place of the old one which pushes V.D. into a dark corner with other unmentionables.

Venereal disease is widely spread throughout the nation's gay communities because society's attitudes toward V.D. generally and homosexuality in particular are both ignorant and intolerant. Gay liberation organizations have been fighting VD ignorance for years, with pamphlets, referrals to doctors, clinics and other means. Even so, there are still doctors who'll refuse to check or treat men whom they think are homosexuals. These "medical" men should be reported to one's local gay liberation organization so that they can be "persuaded" to join in the battle against germs.

In almost every state and city, however, the Department of Public Health provides adequate, although not necessarily superior facilities for VD checkups. If a private sympathetic doctor (ask your local gay organization for his name, since there are at least a few in every locale) can be found, it is wise to ask him to provide oral and anal smears as well as a blood test. Those who worry about anonymity need not do so, since the health departments in each state realize that keeping names a secret is essential if they are to eradicate venereal disease. Honesty with one's doctor is also essential.

VD symptoms are not always clear. For example, it is possible to carry both syphilis and gonorrhea unknowingly for many months. Either disease can cause irreparable harm to one's system. Syphilis can sometimes be spotted by chancres (small sores usually appearing near the genitals or mouth). However, they sometimes appear on other parts of the body too.

Syphilis is best detected through regular blood tests. Often there are no symptoms at all for anal or oral gonorrhea. A regular smear test is therefore wise. Anal VD does not show up in a blood test.

In any case, true shame lies not in contracting VD but in failing to get checkups at regular intervals. One protects not only oneself but one's loved ones too. The theme song on TV's award-winning program, *VD Blues,* was "Don't Give a Dose to the One You Love Most."

·

IMPOTENCE

Dear Lige and Jack,
I am a fifty-three-year-old bachelor and have some kind of mental block which makes me weak sexually.

I was wondering if you could recommend someone who would give me a series of treatments with LSD to try to resolve this mental block and restore my potency.

> Sincerely,
> Martin D.
> Orlando, Florida

Dear Martin,
Impotence, if it has no physiological basis, can be caused by self-imposed mental blocks, and it's true that LSD has been

127

known to help men bypass such psychological states. But don't assume that LSD will solve all problems. If you are causing yourself unnecessary anxiety in the midst of sex, try to understand that you are experiencing the results of fruitless speculations: of giving undue attention to what *may* happen or what has *just* happened. Such concerns have no place in sex—a form of play—easily interrupted by rigid analyzing.

Through your local alternate press or through youthful graduate students who are studying to be psychotherapists, perhaps you can locate a physician who'll use LSD in therapy. But LSD treatment is rare, and is used in research only in certain parts of the country.

●

CURIOSITIES OR FEELINGS?

Dear Friends,

First, excuse my English . . . I'm a Frenchman and I can't write good English!

I'm twenty-one years old and I'm right now a patient in an Army hospital. Reasons: Well, I tried to get my Americanization [citizenship]. I got it, and it cost me my right leg. I lost it in Viet-Nam. . . .

This letter is just because I read your article about "Homosexual Heritage" by Lige and Jack, and it said that you will answer any questions. Here are my questions.

I have never had intercourse with a gay guy, but the point is that I would like to have one. Does that mean that I'm a homosexual or is it just plain curiosity? I have a girl friend and I love her and want to marry her but I've heard a lot of conversations about intercourse with gay guys and they said that they do things wonderful and that they know their thing.

128

Hope to get your answer soon and I hope that you were able to understand this letter.

Truly,
N.C.
New Brunswick, New Jersey

Dear N.C.,
Where did you hear those conversations about how gay guys really know their "thing?" It would seem you've been curious for some time. Well, the fact is, there are some men who know more than others—as is true in all population samplings. We suspect you may be hesitant to follow your natural curiosities because of what others may label you. If you're afraid that drawing close to someone of your own sex would result in your being called unbearable names, then forget the joy of male companionship, if you can, and give up your inalienable right to be affectionate according to your own lights.

If you love your girl friend and want to marry her, what do you want gay guys for? Not lengthy, loving relationships, evidently, but sex—occasioned not by affection but by curiosity. Very well. Enjoy your body. We won't knock curiosity, but we'll remind you that "gay guys," as you call them, have feelings too . . . in case you care. If you got one pregnant, would you marry him?

Labels such as *heterosexual* or *homosexual* don't fit unless you choose them for yourself or unless your emotional and sexual lives are facing only one direction. Your desires seem to be simply sexual and perhaps you may be one of those lucky people who can bypass "homo" and "hetero" prefixes before touching the bodies close to you. It's a fine quality if you've got it, since body formations (gender, size, height, weight) aren't important in our relationships—it's just that we've been reared with culturally imposed ideas of beauty.

• • •

STRAIGHT HOMOSEXUALS

It isn't always easy to spot a person, particularly in gay circles, who carries smelly conventions around with him like abominations in his britches. Today's climate (whether produced by the establishment or by so-called sex revolutionaries) has created a whole army of irresolute spectators. They don't have the guts to *live*—as Agnes Gooch once did—and are floundering around on the edges of living, privately damning those who seem to be enjoying themselves. These people say scarcely a word to anybody, lest they betray the fact that they're not *cool*.

Cool types are afraid to register their opinions for fear they'll seem outdated. Ashamed of their religious scruples or shocked by sexual emancipation, they keep their turmoil to themselves. Honesty might be better served, really, if we would all admit that we're not, not one of us, as familiar with the ways of the world as we'd like to appear to be. A *cool* exterior saves us from questions and commitment.

A person who observes goings-on in the gay subculture that are new or strange to him, and yet shows no outward signs of perplexity, is usually reacting inwardly. These reactions, instead of being based on a wider perspective, can spring from the morality absorbed at some priest's knee. A man can look *cool*, while his palms sweat, clutching a crucifix. Or, if he isn't a victim of centuries-old institutions, the more recent "sexual revolution" has made sexual ignorance such a social "sin" that he's scared to ask

130

honest questions. If only he'd show his true colors, the opinions of prudes and doomsayers—affecting his every move—might soon give way to healthy optimism.

COMING OUT LATE

Dear Lige and Jack,

I'm a gay male, thirty-eight years old, who finally came out of the closet about two and a half years ago. Prior to that time my sole sexual outlet was solitary masturbation (in the prone position) induced by contemplation of beautifully built musclemen. Since becoming overtly gay I've enjoyed my sexual relationships intensely and have no guilt feelings about them, but am troubled by the fact that while I am able to bring my partners to orgasm by fellatio, I am not myself able to come by being blown. I do not desire anal relations. I can only reach climax after a prolonged period of full body contact, and then only when my partner turns me on visually.

What I would like to know is whether this problem of impotence, in regard to oral sex, is a fairly common problem or not? Was it perhaps caused by my late coming out? Can anything be done to overcome it? I am hopeful that my problem, if it proves to be irremediable, will not stand in the way of achieving a permanent love relationship, which must have a basis much

131

stronger than mere sexual attraction and which I most ardently desire.

Sincerely,
Russell, N.
Boston, Massachusetts

Dear Russell,
Gautama Buddha said: ''We are what we think, having become what we thought.'' Your inability to reach a climax when you're being orally stimulated is due, in part, to the extreme caution you've shown through the years. You take hesitant steps, and perhaps you must learn self-abandon, which might be described as throwing your mind/body onto clouds of adventure when you're in bed. Be less precise about your sexual preferences and show yourself a new quality: be explorative.

●

AGEIST WAITERS

Dear Lige and Jack,
We are lovers (GM's) who happen to be ages 22 and 34. Since we dine out quite often we find it particularly aggravating that waiters, especially in gay restaurants, tend to give the check to the elder of us. We always share expenses equally. We feel this is usually a thoughtless assumption, rather than bitchiness, on the part of the waiters, and hope this letter will set them straight (if you'll pardon the expression).

We thank you,
C.S. and C.H.
Phoenix, Arizona

Dear GM's (that's Genital Males, we presume),

If a waiter's thoughtless assumption is the most aggravating thing that happens to you guys, you're in enviable shape! There are four courses of action open to you: (1) Confront the waiter with his ageism. Smile and say, "We're both big boys, honey chile." (2) Start an organization to fight discrimination because of age—with a special consciousness-raising mission to waiters. (3) Decide that the aggravation you experience is making you unnecessarily nervous and try to steer your anger toward the alleviation of some more devastating social injustice. (4) Eat at home.

• • •

AGING

Age is often a mental state. It is an attitude that frequently becomes evident at an early age and there are more than a few young men who at age twenty have already surrendered to attitudes which make them hesitant, feeble, opinionated, stiff, stingy and pious. Their young bodies reflect their attitudes; hence, they never really feel the glory or the passion of being young.

On the other hand there are men in their forties, fifties and upward who have a high sense of adventure and whose manner indicates curiosity and humor. They say "yes" to life and are open, generous and optimistic as a result. They have cared for their bodies, and this care has paid off in high spirits, zest and gracefulness. In short they are beautiful.

Age, therefore, has little meaning if it is thought about in the conventional way. Someone who magnifies the significance of precise birth dates (and there are many who suffer this affliction) shows that he's attached to superficial data. How many times do young men, upon meeting one another ask, as a near opener, "How old are you?" The questioner shows himself ignorant of many true secrets with this question. He should be able to know, simply by feeling the vibrations of a new friend, whether or not he'll make exciting companion or lover no matter what his age. There are far too many who take a shallow approach to age and who cut off a new relationship before it's begun, simply because a man's age does not fit preconceived notions and silly preferences.

As for those who refer to "aunties" and who are openly hostile to men because of their advanced age, these are, in our book, beneath contempt. They show not only that they are cruel, insecure, thoughtless and ugly, but that they themselves are elderly in the most negative sense, even though they be ever so young.

WELL ROUNDED

Dear People,

Although I cannot say that I am particularly fond of the label, I am what is so quaintly called a "chubby." (Surely someone can come up with a better term? "Chubby" suggests a pooh-like quality that some of us just aren't able to maintain with any kind of dignity.) This is not to say that I am "fat"; that word has a quality of flabbiness that doesn't fit me. Nevertheless, I am a well-rounded individual who, although married, finds an interest in men of various sizes, shapes and colors.

Now I am not suggesting a "Fat Power" move (although it would have a certain following). But occasionally I'd like to see something printed that could be useful and informative for the person who looks a little more Rubensesque than Michelangelic.

When I first arrived in New York I was told that this was the land of the "chubby chaser." (Ugh!) Well, I have been cruising the streets and bending the lampposts for months to no avail.

> Sincerely,
> Thomas E.
> New York, New York

Dear Thomas,
It is true that New York is possibly the only city in the nation that has supported—at various times—an all-male bar wherein you Rubensesque fellows are pursued by men with a preference for your proportions. Check with the city's gay organizations and someone will direct you to the newest "chubby chaser's" bar or to the latest social.

●

YESTERDAY'S PIONEERS

Dear Lige and Jack,
Many years ago, when I still worked in North Carolina, we had an active clan of gays and we didn't really try to sustain our identity. I am all for our rights and will do most anything I can to help us maintain them. . . . But . . . and it is a big but . . . I just

135

am not too sure that this "force" and continued demonstrations are the right way. I just happen to believe that some of us back in the dark ages (and believe you me they were the years that you didn't dare let on that you slept with another male) actually helped bring about this new "betterment" for us gays.

I regret to say that I still can't come out at work and say to the boss that I'm gay, but I don't go around playing with the gals anymore either. I live my life with my lover and I enjoy being with all my gay friends, but I have lots of straight friends who, I am sure, know about Jimmy and me, but we don't discuss it, nor do I intend to flaunt in their faces that I think I am different. I don't really. I think I am just as normal as they, only I love a guy, and I'm a guy. Why must people always make things so hard for themselves?

> Fondly,
> Lew S.
> Chicago, Illinois

Dear Lew,
You've an independent streak that makes you not "different" but unique in a very positive way. You realize that the past and the present lean into each other. You also see that yesterday's pioneers made today's life-styles possible. Many of those pioneers worked cleverly and effectively from their closets, developing formulas to expand today's freedoms.

●

SAGITTA

Dear Jack and Lige,
In 1918, the First World War ended. For Germany, this meant

Revolution and Social Democracy. Being 16 years old, and having been brought up there, I felt these to be exciting times. The Kaiser had run away to Holland. According to the press of the period, he had had homosexual affairs during his reign, and there were suicides in connection with them.

The newborn Republic, headed by Friedrich Ebert, intended to make many needed, drastic changes in government. Professor Magnus Hirschfeld, a leading middle-aged M.D. in Berlin, took advantage of the new political developments. He formed an organization to liberate homosexuals, and strived to have Paragraph 175 (regarding sodomy) eliminated from German law. The idea spread like wildfire all through Germany, and soon branches were established in most big cities.

By 1920, it was an undeniable fact that I belonged to what is now, in America, called the Gay World. At age 18, I was the youngest leader of one such group in my hometown. We named it *Sagitta* (Arrow), for a very brilliant start. Having had 50 paying members, as we did, was a feat in those days in a small community.

In 1926, 24 years old, I arrived on American soil, and went sexually, as most respectable people of my type did then, into hiding. My experiences since then have been many: cops, blackmail, rough-trade-holdups, disease, courts, psychiatrists looking for a way out, 30 years of unhappy and unsuccessful marriage, you-name-it, I had it.

What a different life the homosexual youth of today can have. Everything is open, and thanks to daring people like you, there is a still better future ahead.

As for generation gaps, that is a lot of crap. If people of all ages and walks of life would only take a bit of trouble trying to understand one another, they would find out how much more common ground they have to make life a richer, happier and more rewarding experience.

It gives me great satisfaction at my advanced age to read your script and see that more and more people care. Eventually even lawmakers?

Yours truly,
Bernard P.
Waco, Texas

Dear Bernard,
You say that people of all ages and walks of life should take trouble to understand each other, and this captures a great essence of ideal endeavor. Men with your perspective can help us all bridge so-called "generation gaps."

● ● ●

TRAITS

The effects of discrimination which have reigned so long over the gay community are subtly pernicious. Like all members of minority groups, gay women and men may be likely to develop certain traits because of social pressures. Many may erect ego defenses or become obsessively concerned with their "differentness." Some are hypersensitive to every remark lest it betray prejudice. A few deny affiliation with those who share their desires and withdraw from their society altogether, unhappy and resentful.

All homosexuals recognize traits such as these in at least a few of their gay associates. To some degree most *do* suffer from what they think is the necessity to hide and disguise their deepest feelings. Despite these pressures there are many mature men and women who've mustered the strength to overcome such socially induced obstacles.

Doing so has made them stronger individuals and has saved many from developing distorted personalities.

WHERE SHALL WE PUT
MOM?

Dear Lige and Jack,
Next month my mother is coming to visit for a few days. She doesn't know I'm gay and she's never met my lover, who I'm presently living with. My lover is pretty uptight about having her stay (sleep) here and wants to put her in a hotel although we have the space available for her comfort. He says we'll have her over for dinner and entertain her royally. I don't want to hurt anyone's feelings; what do you guys do?

Anxiously yours,
Edward T.
Cleveland, Ohio

Dear Edward,
Jack's mother sleeps on our king-sized bed when she visits and we bed down on a floor mat in the living room. Why is your lover uptight? He hasn't got anything to be ashamed of in front

of your Mom, does he? Is he afraid she'll *find out*? If you don't want to tell your mother about your life simply take care not to hold hands when she's around, stop playing knees under the dining table and it seems sure that unless your lover says: "Madam, I'd like you to know that I bugger your son with an affectionate regularity," she probably won't catch on.

If your lover just can't get himself together for her visit, maybe *he* should stay in a hotel. So far it's *his* problem, not yours and not hers.

•

LONG-DISTANCE
LOVE

Dear Sirs,

In July, 1970, I met here in New York a young man from Austria, Rudolf, and fell in love with him. Our initial meeting, like so many gay encounters, was brief, but we corresponded faithfully for twelve months, until finally we were able to make our dream come true. Rudolf returned to me last July and we have been very happy together since then. I can truly say that I would ask nothing more of life but to continue our relationship.

The problem is that Rudolf, lacking any occupational skill that would have qualified him for immigration to the United States, had to enter on a tourist visa. His present visa expires in April, but we expect to be able to get another three-month extension.

If my lover and I were of opposite sexes, there would be no difficulty—we could be married and he could obtain the status of a permanent resident. Because we are gay it looks as though the government will eventually separate us.

We now have at least three, maybe six months in which to

act. Rudolf and I want to remain together and will go anywhere and do anything we must to achieve this end.

Can you help us, or can you direct us to anyone else who might?

Very truly yours,
David L.
Elmhurst, New York

Dear David,

(1) Talk with an immigration lawyer.

(2) Find out about Rudolf's attending a specialized school or college in the United States in order for him to obtain a student's visa.

(3) Consider the case of a British friend of ours who married an American friend who happened to be a girl. She knew him to be gay and enjoyed his company enough to put a "Mrs." in front of her name for at least two years. If he remains married for two years he becomes a permanent resident and can apply for U.S. citizenship. In the meantime his visa allows him to work.

(4) Finally, you could always move to Austria. Whatever you do, remember what Deborah sang: "Be brave, young lovers."

●

HOW DO I TELL HIM?

Dear Heads,

I'm eighteen years old and have been out for two years. I recently was introduced to a twenty-two-year-old who is also gay. I've met him several times now and have fallen in love with

141

him. My problem is I don't know how he feels toward me. I want very much to tell him what I feel, but I don't know how since I've never fallen in love before. What can I do to show him how much I care?

Yours,
Gerald S.
Washington, D.C.

Dear Gerald,
If you continue seeing each other, without making demands on each other, you'll know how to tell him you care. Flash those big baby eyes at him, smile till your gums hurt. Who knows, maybe he'll tell you first!

●

WANTED: A MARRIAGE CEREMONY

Dear Lige and Jack,
My lover and I are planning on a gay marriage in the near future. We would like to know if there is any church in the State of New York that would perform our ceremony. Any information would be greatly appreciated.

Sincerely yours,
Russell D.
Elmira, New York

Dear Russell,
Check with clergymen from a few liberal churches, such as the Unitarian-Universalists, the Congregationalists, and maybe

even an Episcopalian or two. Your search will assist, perhaps, in educating a few men of the cloth. Be sure to call on them wearing a tie.

There are also "gay churches"—both Catholic and Protestant—in Manhattan and elsewhere. Check the city's gay guides to find their listings.

•

ALTERNATE CULTURE

Dear Guys,
I would like to see articles written on homosexuality in the rock world. I know we have many brothers in the rock scene, though often closeted.

I would also like to see articles on "alternate culture" for gays. I myself come from one of those "hippie" communes and am having considerable problems relating to the gay scene (i.e., bars, cruising and baths).

In closing, you're a great inspiration in my keeping the closet door open. Continue to be progressive and never forget to smile . . . do it a whole bunch!

> Love,
> David B.
> Cleveland, Ohio

Dear David,
We *do* have many "brothers and sisters" in the rock scene, and not only among performers but among managers and promoters too. Brian Epstein, the deceased manager of the Beatles, was only one of the many homosexually inclined geniuses in the business. Janis Joplin is said to have had several female lovers,

143

according to a biography by her friend, Peggy Caserta, entitled *Going Down With Janis*.

But a "brother" or "sister" isn't just someone who shares your sexual orientation. It is someone who cherishes freedoms and liberties, or values sentiments and laughter as you do. Don't look for a singer's homosexuality or you'll miss out on what's good. Look for life-attitude—for humanity.

If you're having trouble adjusting to gay bars, baths, etc., you are one of many sensitive people who do. All sensitive "straights" have trouble relating to their clubs too. The din, the glitter, and the crowds are distracting and often tacky. Somewhere, though, perhaps in another locale, or in a gay organization, or on the beach, you'll meet men with whom you'll click, and when you do, you'll look at "alternate culture" and "straight culture" and will say, "I must create my own culture, because no group finally satisfies me with what it offers."

Don't rule out current-day social spas altogether. Just don't spend your life in them.

•

HAIRPINS

Gentlemen,
I have a friend, who lets remarks drop, like, "Oh they have a gay-bar address book." He checks all the male baskets and sits on the couch in such a position that his basket actually sticks out. I let him read gay books; he says he doesn't like them, but never turns one down.

When we slept in the same motel room (twin beds) he kept a solid hard-on all the time. I invited myself to his bed, saying, "I don't like the term used by society of sex with the same sex, but I enjoy it." He never would let me join him.

How can I get him in bed? He's thirty-one years old, never

144

married, never dates (females or males), plays tennis, golf and
bridge.

Andrew J.
Decatur, Alabama

Dear Andrew,
You like challenging games, yes? At least it seems your emotions aren't involved. You just want to turn a long chase into a
good lay, right? Your friend, it seems, is known in "straight"
terminology as a "prick teaser." He's also locked in his closet.
Stop worrying about this clod and you'll relax enough to throw
humor into the situation—jokes that'll make him feel at ease.
Why not introduce nude wrestling as an addition to bridge, golf
and tennis?

Here's hoping you enjoy him when you finally get him in the
sack. Usually men who dig the chase aren't interested in a
second round of festivities. After success, the mystery is gone.
Why don't you try to make it with someone you really admire
instead. Your contempt for this fellow is obvious. In fact,
maybe he senses it and therefore keeps you at a respectable
distance.

● ● ●

INNOCENCE

Nobody, except maybe a hustler, likes to look dumb. Yet
there are plenty of people who don't want to seem too
smart either. They're afraid they'll lose what they think is
one of their more attractive traits: innocence.

The man who *tries* to look innocent and the man who
seeks such a look are both hung up in the virginity syn-

drome. The facts of life, particularly if these have included the enjoyment of a full sex life, disturb them. They value ignorance, failing to see that their behavior is ostrich-like.

As absurd as it may seem, there are actually lots of men who run about in Turkish baths trying to find sex partners who haven't yet had sex. They want to be *the first*.

HE'S 50, I'M 20!

Dear Jack and Lige,
We have a question. Larry and I are in love. We've lived together for three years but we do not interest each other sexually.

We have our home, a dog and bank account together but not sex. What does this symbolize? Do we still consider each other lovers? Larry is fifty and I am twenty.

> Sincerely,
> Ricky and Larry
> San Francisco, California

Dear Ricky and Larry,
The word "lover" is much abused. Such a label isn't important—it's how you treat those you love that counts. Some

lovers don't even live together . . . and yet they love each other passionately and are together often.

Age, position, pets and bank accounts are superficial props. They mean nothing. To insure independence, however, you may wish to keep your finances separate. This way, you, at twenty, will have a chance to build your own securities.

Reference is made to your sex life, or, perhaps, to the lack of it. We love others in our lives with whom we have no sex, don't we? Let's just hope your lover sees that you have the freedom to be horny—unless, of course, you're not interested in sex, and then it doesn't matter.

Enjoy life with your friend but make new friends, together and separately—not for sex, necessarily, but for your own wider perspectives.

•

SHOULD I BEHAVE?

Dear Lige and Jack,
I am gay and have had a lover for four years. We live together and have done so since we met. I love him very much and I wouldn't like the idea of losing him.

He sometimes works nights and my question is this: Should I stay home and wait till he's in my arms again or should I go out? To a movie, a gay bar? Should I behave myself?

> Yours truly,
> Joseph D.
> Hartford, Connecticut

Dear Joseph,
Of course you shouldn't behave yourself, silly! Go out any-

where you like. But there will be many times, probably, when it'll be most fun waiting for him at home. ''Behaving'' means you're holding yourself in check. As long as you're not hurting anybody, why should you behave?

● ● ●

UNCHECKED EXPLORATION

Gay people frighten conventional men and women for the same reasons that orthodox religionists are frightened by heretics and freethinkers.

The freedoms allowed by gay culture are open-ended. There is no telling where unchecked exploration and curiosity will lead.

Many gay people, however, contrary to what their "straight" neighbors think, aren't any more daring or experimental than those neighbors themselves. Too many don't realize—unfortunately—that they're free to abandon all sexual dogmas and rituals and to go wherever curiosity takes them—to examine every hidden corner of experience as long as they do not trample on the freedoms of others.

While gay culture enjoys the flair of many incredulous and original minds, it could use still more. Gay people have elbow room, after all, to fly out to the fringes, to the farthest perimeters of human encounter. They may uncover forbidden joys as their minds encompass and pass beyond socially defined limits.

Taboos, restrictions, ceremonies and assumptions fall flat under more critical eyes in gay circles. Many gay men and women laugh at the social absurdities they discover. Many sense that the tendencies of dominant majorities toward self-congratulation and their overriding beliefs in their own superiority are as hollow.

The fact that many gay people can see through customs, formalities and rules not only alarms sexual conformists but may make them uncomfortable in the face of such scrutiny.

While it is sad that there are so many people too insecure to cope with the presence of emotional and sexual freedom in their midst, this should never inhibit or delay the development of freedom, curiosity and exploration in gay communities.

UNSPECIFIED INVITE

Dear Jack and Lige,
We would like to have you for dinner and drinks sometime. It won't be for a while yet as we are remodeling our apartment; but you are welcome in our home anytime.

> With fondest regards,
> Jon and Michael
> Elizabeth, New Jersey

Dear Jon and Michael,
We've never met you, but thanks for the dinner invite. We're

vegetarians. No meat please! In fact you'd better mail us a menu in advance. No drinks either, or at least not those which are poisoned by alcohol or carbonation. As soon as your apartment has been remodeled, set the date. We'll be expecting your chauffeur around eight.

• • •

LOVERS

Relationships thrive best in an atmosphere of personal freedom. It is only when one partner or another imposes his particular design on life that *individuality* (and the joy experienced when a lover feels appreciated for his own personality) is crushed. Under an arrangement in which one partner's "trip" is paramount and in which he becomes a director, spontaneity fades and a certain prearranged style takes its place. One lover accepts and the other dispenses: sooner or later this arrangement is bound to extract a toll. The "leader" may begin to wonder if his lover has a mind of his own, and may go looking for someone whom he admires for taking more initiative. Or the less assertive of the two may grow tired of following directions and seek for himself a partner who'll appreciate him for his own qualities.

Most people do their "best" as they see it, although it is not always obvious to others, particularly when those others have a preconceived notion of what constitutes "the best." Lovers must make a special effort to find out enough about one another so that whatever is truly important to each becomes clear. Once this happens, a partner can begin to understand what's "best" from his lover's stand-point. The result is not only a fuller appreciation of the intricacies of another being but a positive response from that person as well.

This means that neither partner must lean *thoughtlessly* for support on the other. There are times when anyone must take a rest and it's part of the comfort of a close relationship that both partners feel free to do so if necessary. But a temporary arrangement mustn't become a life-style and even if there's an equitable division of labor, both partners should make sure they're capable of making their own way in the world outside the home. A loving union assures that each member is self-regulating so that if one partner or the other withdraws or dies, the other will be equipped with his own strengths.

I DON'T WANT TO
LOSE HIM

Dear Fellows,

Almost a year ago I met a beautiful guy, the same age as I am (twenty-two), very beautiful with a terrific personality. After a short time we decided to become lovers. All was well until a month ago when I found out that he's been sleeping with other guys. At this point I don't know what to do. I love him very much and don't want to lose him. He claims he also loves me and that the others mean nothing to him. I don't understand why I can't satisfy him. What can I do to keep us from breaking up?

Yours truly,
Gerald S.
Boston, Massachusetts

Dear Gerald,
1. Don't pester him with jealous questions.
2. Don't assume that he doesn't love you.
3. Accept him as he is, rather than as you'd have him be.
4. Ask him to accept you as you are. That's fair, ain't it?
5. Don't sit at home and wait for him.
6. Don't build your life around him only.
7. Develop closer ties to friends and be sure to make lots of new ones.
8. Tell him that you're glad he loves you, no matter what he does in his spare time, and that both of you will benefit from your new, daring, explorative and free relationship.
9. Invite him to enjoy the company of your friends too.
10. Realize that your letter to us shows a false dualism when it divides "beauty" and "personality." Personality/character is what creates beauty.

●

IT'S WHAT'S UP FRONT
THAT COUNTS

Dear Guys,
I'm turning to you desperately with a ridiculous problem. I'm a butch-bi, extremely romantic guy who rarely makes out be-

152

cause I'm attracted to a very rare type. Now that I've finally found him, I don't know what to do. In a current cigarette ad there's an unbelievably beautiful guy holding a bowling ball next to a broken cigarette. I can't get him out of my mind! I know this is stupid, but can you suggest how I can meet him without making a fool of myself?

Gio from Jersey

Dear Gio,
Call the cigarette company's advertising agency and ask for his name. Tell them you've got a ''modeling'' job for him to do and that your cigarette is a silly millimeter longer.

●

SUFFOCATING ENTANGLEMENTS

Dear Lige and Jack,
I just recently came out and on my first visit to a gay bar I met and went home with someone. After a week of seeing him, he professed his love for me. Although I like my friend as well as anyone I have ever met, I do not love him and have told him so repeatedly. As I'm new to the gay life, I feel that I should meet and have sex with a variety of people before deciding if I want to take a lover. My friend says that he doesn't want anyone but me, and although it will hurt him, he will accept the fact that I may have relations with others. Unbeknownst to him, I have met another fellow who I also like and have slept with. My new friend has not come right out and said so, but I feel he too is beginning to think in more serious terms. Is it possible in the gay life to establish more than one deep friend sex relationship

153

concurrently? I see the next couple of years as exciting ones if I can avoid suffocating entanglements.

Yours truly,
Brad T.
Washington, D.C.

Dear Brad,
Not only in the "gay life" is it possible to enjoy more than one relationship, but this should be so in *any* life. Don't follow other folks' social norms—gay or straight—*establish your own!*

Lovers should encourage one another to be free to come and go. Where real freedom exists, it is appreciated and is seldom abused.

Could it be possible that your friends are overly serious because you want them to be? Be sure you're open and honest with them.

•

BOOZER BLUES

Dear Jack and Lige,
I live with a talented and marvelous man and have for four years. He's so thoughtful, when he's sober anyway. Occasionally he gets on a real "binge." I wouldn't mind so much but he gets violent and negative and always wants to start a fight. Not just with me but with friends too. He seems to be getting worse lately and makes it harder for me to be around him. I can't talk him into not drinking. How can I help him with this and not hurt myself too?

Please reply.
Leland E.
Cincinnati, Ohio

154

Dear Leland,

Go to local Alcoholics Anonymous meetings and ask for literature on the subject. Listen to the best advice of men and women who've preserved their relationships under trying circumstances. In some larger cities there are gay A.A. groups. If possible, see if your lover will go to a counselor—someone in whom he has confidence. In any case, if he starts drinking, remove yourself and friends from his company until he regains his composure. You are not abandoning him under such circumstances, but simply putting him on notice that you're not a willing punching bag. Show some self-respect by taking a powder and maybe he'll get the message.

●

MENTAL MASOCHISM

Dear Jack and Lige,

Last October I met a gay usher at a wedding. Since then, we've seen each other several times. The problem is I haven't seen or heard from him for over a month. I wrote a letter to this guy, telling him how I feel toward him; I saw him three days later and all he said was he had received the letter. Since that night I haven't heard from him. I love this guy very much and I need him. I see him once, then I don't hear from him for two months. I can't stand it this way. What the hell should I do? Should I call him? Should I try to forget him, even though that would be painful?

> Sincerely,
> Arthur F.
> Stamford, Connecticut

Dear Arthur,

Yeah, forget him. You wrote your letter to let him know how

155

you feel. The next step was his and he didn't take it. Please don't feel sorry for yourself either. Take stock of yourself, count your many assets and set out to make new friends. Next time, before you "fall in love," make sure you've chosen a more responsive lover.

●

"I HAVE MANY PURSUERS"

Dearest Lige and Jack,
I am sixteen years old and I think highly of the "gay life."

Due to the fact that I am so young and (modestly saying) extremely good-looking, I have many pursuers. Please answer or comment on the following:

1. Should I keep my lover and play around or should I drop my lover and play around . . . even though I love him (my lover) most sincerely?

2. Other than the actual sexual acts, how should I prove my love to my partner?

Most sincerely,
Alfred R.
Jamaica, New York

Dear Alfred,
It is more important to think highly of life itself than to think highly of "gay life" in particular. Gay life is part of life and is a much happier affair if we've learned to think highly—period. Whenever you hear folks knocking "gay" life you will realize that they've made a nonexistent distinction.

Should you keep your lover and play around? Why not ask your lover if it's OK with him? As an honest person, you don't mean that you'd "play around" behind his back, do you? And what, exactly, do you mean by "play around?" Does that nebulous phrase describe the level on which your personal relationships take place?

There's certainly no reason why you shouldn't enjoy the company of many friends, male *and* female, if that's what you'd like to do. Your lover would want you to be satisfied and happy, wouldn't he? He wouldn't want you to feel confined or trapped.

If you love him, as you say, "most sincerely," help him to take part in your life, to meet and get to know your new friends too. Enjoy them together for *sound* reasons.

If you want him to know he's loved, there are many ways you can do so. Make him feel more secure by showing a genuine interest in his life and in the things that interest him. Encourage him to develop his talents, to become himself, as he should help you to do the same.

If you are well suited to each other and can still laugh together, months or even years from now, it will be because you've both been honest and have *built* a good relationship.

Each of you, though, should maintain his individuality. Be your own best selves and pursue your own values.

•

REBEL AND YANKEE COOKING

Dear Lige and Jack,
This will no doubt sound trivial to you but to me it's important at the moment. Such a small thing shouldn't interfere with a relationship but I'm beginning to pick up hostile vibes from my lover.

We've been taking turns fixing dinner once or twice a week. He invariably fixes something that he knows I dislike with a passion. Our backgrounds are different and we were reared on different diets (Southern cooking and New York delicacies). He's even done several repeats of dishes I've requested him not to. I've thought of doing the same thing to him but he'll eat most anything and I'm not into playing games. Any advice would be appreciated. I'm stumped.

Sincerely,
Franklin E.
New York, New York

Dear Franklin,
Taste is a matter of taste, and there's no accounting for it . . . although many people hope that by giving repeated exposures to loved ones and friends they can convert them to "the better way." It's not necessarily a hostile act, but well-intentioned zeal which is often unconscious. Maybe your lover is trying to expand your tastes or perhaps he's only cooking what he knows best.

If you don't like it, don't eat it. He'll get the message. Or, if subtlety is a *must*, roll on the floor and agonize about acute indigestion.

• • •

UNWARRANTED ANXIETY

Unwarranted anxiety springs from either memory or anticipation. If it springs from memory, it has arisen from one's own limited perception of what has happened —since no individual perspective is complete, no past event can be remembered or grasped in its entirety. Whatever seemed to have happened would be described quite differently by each person who participated. Therefore, dwelling on past events—if they cause anxiety—is masochistic.

If anxiety springs from anticipation, it has its source in something that hasn't yet taken place. Only a mind that is asking for anxiety bothers itself with worries about events which haven't yet occurred.

The crown of anxiety is speculation.

A person who speculates about the past or the future is playing a mind game. Speculation misses what is really happening because it is concerned with possibilities.

There is only one way to meet what is really happening and that is to deal with what is really happening *now*, at this very moment.

Until a moment arrives it cannot be met.

If the mind is clogged with unwarranted anxieties it can't effectively encounter the circumstances of the present.

•

LATIN LOVER

Dear Ones,

Fortunately or unfortunately I am a lover of Latins. Being a teacher I must be discreet about the whole situation. As you can imagine I'm looking for a Latin lover.

159

Where in the city can a person find respectable Latins who are also "in the life."

Joe F.
Riverhead, New York

Dear Joe,
New York City and its environs is overflowing with gay Latins. Los Angeles has its share of Chicanos. But to seek a lover with such a "qualification" not only limits your chances for a relationship but demonstrates a peculiar imbalance in values. A person's trust, humor, curiosity and warmth should, if you will forgive us for pontificating, transcend your demand for ethnic distinction.

●

NOT LIKE ME

Attn: Lige Clarke or Jack Nichols,
I am writing to ask if you could suggest places where gay men such as myself could meet others but not for sex! If this sounds odd, let me explain:

I belong to a rather large group of gay people who cannot or will not have sex with people of my own class, or age, or intellectual attainments. We need not go into the psychological reasons, but I have no trouble in obtaining all the sex I want by either picking up a hustler, or preferably, a truck driver, construction worker, or anyone of the non-intellectual type. Indeed they often turn out to be as gay as can be, in fact sometimes losing their masculine image, which is disappointing.

I feel there are many gay people like me who would be so glad

160

if they knew a place, a bar, or restaurant, or club where they could meet people just to talk with. Oh yes, I don't mean Mattachine, etc., because again I speak for so many others, I have to be very discreet, I could never join such a "known" society. Can you make any suggestions for businessmen like me (in my fifties) who must put on a front in business, etc., and during these long lonely weekends would like to meet a compatible gay person of similar disposition.

The fact that I sign with first name does not in any way lessen my desire for your opinion. Perhaps someday I shall "come out" but I have children (I live alone and am divorced). My business partners must never know of my predilections. I'm sure you understand.

Sincerely,
Ray
New York City

Dear Ray,
No, quite frankly we don't understand, but then the Declaration of Independence grants you the right to pursue "happiness" your way. Thus far, however, it looks as though you're wallowing in disappointment because you, like some men—both "gay" and "straight"—are seeking "sex objects." Your rigid "relationship" standards doom you to loneliness. How, indeed, do you define "losing" a masculine image? It wouldn't surprise us if this means that your partner suddenly becomes responsive to you and that your guilt feelings about sex allow you to see such responsiveness as reprehensible. Can't you see through "images" to start with—When you first meet a guy? Practice.

The gay organizations you mention are quite discreet. Many have benefited from visits to them. You might too.

161

● ● ●

ROUGH TRADE

Rough Trade is slang for men who are usually large, rough, muscular, non-intellectual and emotionless but who allow themselves the pleasure of being manipulated by other men, while they, being *machos*, do little or nothing. Genuine rough trade is presumed to be heterosexual and generally will behave as though a "blow job" or whatever it is he's getting is something of an imposition on his otherwise rampantly hetero life-style.

Our concern doesn't lie with the psychology of such men but with that of the gay people who are attracted to them.

It seems obvious that those who seek out such men (known in slang as "trade queens") aren't interested in romance, equality, or, particularly, in reciprocation from their he-man partners. Most often, in fact, "trade" is a one-night affair and since such *machos* often carry with them a suppressed contempt for homosexuals, or at least are somewhat impervious to them, there is always an element of danger involved for the gay men who invite their company.

Danger as an element of sexual excitement has its origin in society's condemnation of homosexuality. The man who relishes danger might often be hoping, unconsciously, to be punished for sex acts he considers wrong. At the same time, the sex objects he chooses (who, he hopes, are not homosexually inclined themselves) he considers superior to gay men for much the same reason. There is also a feeling that one has become "one of the guys" by such association or that one has "put one over" on the more dominant group by getting into their pants.

In a relationship between rough trade and a trade queen

there is always an element of subservience. The rough trade is "allowing" the gay man certain liberties with his body but does not return (physically, at least) the interest shown. There is usually little of what is commonly known as romance. If there is, the gay man is usually appreciated primarily for his wit and personality and more often than not for a degree of support, usually financial, which he gives to his "manly" partner. On top of all of this, there exist, as in S&M attitudes, highly stereotyped ideas of what constitutes masculinity. While being a trade queen is anybody's prerogative, some of the facts mentioned herein are worth consideration.

TIED TOGETHER

Dear Lige and Jack,
My lover, Tim, and I have been trying to figure out some way to attach ourselves legally as well as in the eyes of the church (we were married by Rev. Cardell at the First Unitarian Church in Albany). After reading about gay adoption we were wondering if this has been attempted in New York or its courts? If you know of any way my lover, twenty-one, could adopt me, nineteen, please let us know where to inquire about it.

> Sincerely,
> Jeff V.
> Morrisonville, New York

Dear Jeff,

Walt Whitman asks: "Were you looking to be held together by lawyers? or by an agreement on a paper? or by arms? Nay, not the world, nor any living thing, will so cohere."

In any case, if you must, check with a lawyer. Why adoption? Why not a needle and a thread?

●

MEMORY LANE

Dear Lige and Jack,

You've brought to mind a lifelong but separated friendship I've had with Kevin. We first met in fourth grade and couldn't stand each other. Recess was for fighting and he usually got the better of me. But I was determined to beat him and after some months of training, did just that. The animosity melted on the spot and we became good "butch" friends.

Meanwhile, sleeping overnight with friends was considered *de rigueur* in my middle-west climate during grade school and even junior high. No one thought it "queer" until high school (ninth grade). I was with practically all my friends—mutual masturbation, sucking (never fucking for some odd reason) —but never with Kevin.

Finally, in my junior year we were out on a beer bust —everyone supposedly drunk and Kevin pulled me away in the bushes, planted himself firmly on me and kissed me hard and desperately. I know it sounds like something out of a Bronte novel but I'll never forget that kiss. It turned into sex, of course, that night and continued until we both left for college.

Kevin is now married with several handsome children. But whenever I come home, he's there—almost like a "stagedoor Johnny." He says he's never had "adult" sex with another man and somehow I believe him.

164

God, how beautiful he is, just reaching forty, totally masculine, natural athletic body, completely naive about gay life.

My last meeting with Kevin was this spring when I went home for my father's funeral. Afterward close friends were invited to the home. . . . Kevin and family included, among fifty or so.

He came over to me, started to shake my hand—both of us about to cry—and kissed me. Not passionately, I'm sure no one noticed. Then a squeeze of the hand and that's it.

Except to say, I remember his first kiss. And his last . . . and the beauty of it all.

How dull it must sound on paper, but it's one of my happiest memories.

> Best regards,
> A reader

Dear Reader,
It doesn't sound dull on paper at all! Thank you for sharing your memory with us. Perchance Kevin remembers as often as you do.

● ● ●

TENSION IN THE BODY

It was no accident that Walt Whitman celebrated the body and its care more passionately than any other major poet. He saw the connection between any man's state of mind and the healthiness and agility of his body. "That I was," he wrote, "I knew was of my body and what I should be I knew I should be of my body." In another passage he sings: "All comes by the body, only health puts you rapport with the universe."

A healthy body, one that is well cared for and demonstrates the athletic nature of a man, stands as one of his most attractive attributes. As the rushing frustrations of urban life close in upon us, everyone needs time, each day, in fact, to stretch, build, and strengthen the body. By doing so, each man can automatically exude a great deal of physical magnetism. His walk assumes new spring and balance. His carriage shows pride and straightforward zest. His limbs and joints, his hips and wrists fall into a new rhythm, and his clothing does not hide him. As Whitman put it: "The strong sweet quality he has strikes through the cotton and the broadcloth."

Why are so many plagued with tension? Man's body is unable to keep stride with the technology he's creating. Tension, which is very much the product of technology, grows in each person in extremely subtle ways, building itself into the body's structure over the years and turning people into irritable automatons. Posture, carriage and expression demonstrate the evil grip of machine-world living on men's souls.

What happens to them is tragic: they become harnessed to forces operating outside themselves, forces which do not originate from *within*, and they allow these alien compulsions to drag them at unnatural speeds. Thus, instead of relating to fellows on an unaffected, unadulterated level, they respond from a mind/body that has been influenced by artificial persuasions, those manufactured by technology. They move in step with mechanical velocities rather than with nature's easygoing self-actualizing rhythms.

Nature has "primal sanities." "Now I see the secret of the making of the best persons," sang Whitman. "It is to grow in the open air and to eat and sleep with the earth."

Urban men and women must be much more fastidious

today than ever before about making a daily return to quiet meditation in their homes and to caring for their bodies. Yoga and exercise, such as swimming and walking, are needed to combat the quality of city life in a technologically strictured society.

The body must move, not as the slave of outward commands but from its own center. Too many men, when they dance to life, do so not from the inner depths of their bodies but on cue from their extremities. Instead of being in command of themselves they seem to be disjointed and frantic. To feel whole again they must return to the body and feel the quiet pulsations of its individualistic beat.

SLEEPTALKER

Dear Sirs,

I live in a town with a population of seven hundred and everything and everyone is straight. Lately everyone has been asking me when I am going to get married or else when I am going to get a girl friend. I'm running out of excuses (usually I say I've been dating a girl from another town). But now they want to know when I'm going to bring her home. I'm really stumped. Girls want to go out with me too. I'm in the National Guard and at night when I'm asleep I talk. Guys try to hear me but they can't make out what I say, thank God. I know what I'm saying

167

but I hide it. I've been pretty good at hiding it so far. It's usually a dream about one of the troopers. I'm afraid it's going to slip or be revealed in some way. The worst thing about it is I have never even touched a guy—or a girl, as far as that goes—in my whole twenty years' existence. I thought about taking sleeping pills and ending it all but then I think of all the fun I could have with another guy. But where I live there are none. Then again on the other hand I'd like to have a wife and kids. Really screwed up, don't you think? A gay life is scandalous and easily black-mailed. That's what I'm afraid of. I am really undecided as to what I should do or to whom I should turn for advice. Please tell me what you think. I'll be waiting impatiently.

Sincerely yours,
Tom G.
Illinois

Dear Tom,
You're letting everyone else make decisions for you. Your craving for respectibility costs you a lot! Why not travel to a nearby city? You're twenty years old. Explore! Question! Be a little more patient. Blackmail is rare. You don't have to follow anyone else's pattern. Set your own.

•

HOW YA GONNA KEEP 'EM
DOWN ON THE FARM?

Dear Lige and Jack,
I am a gay male almost forty years old, very lonely, frustrated and sometimes thinking of suicide. There was never a chance in

my life to have contact with another male. This town and most areas around here are almost 100 percent straight. After ten years of marriage, which was almost hell, we broke up and my ex-wife and three children moved to Florida. There is only one person who knows about my gay desires and that is a psychiatrist who treated me for a nervous breakdown. After a few sessions with him I was ready for another breakdown.

It is impossible for me to move into the big city because of my past conservative life. To put it plainly, I would be afraid.

About twice a year some straight friends take me along to New York City where I pick up a few magazines and newspapers but with extreme care. There is never a chance to meet another gay male.

How can I contact other gay males without being exposed to my straight friends?

Karl,
Elizabeth, Pennsylvania

Dear Karl,
Why do you go to New York only with "straight" friends? Really, mister, you're a big boy now and you can visit the city by yourself.

Give yourself a chance to meet other gay males. Sounds like you're blocking yourself so that you don't have opportunities to do as you'd wish.

And what kind of friends do you have? Jack's Mom once defined a friend as someone in front of whom one can think aloud. Perhaps a definition like that might help you to search for new levels in your friendships.

●

I WON'T REBUILD MY
CLOSET

The following letter was received after the victory of Richard Nixon over George McGovern in 1972, prior to the eruption of the Watergate scandals. McGovern, during the 1972 primaries, spoke on behalf of civil liberties for homosexuals. Prior to the election his Manhattan campaign office placed a half-page ad in the newspaper we edited.

Dear Guys,
The election is over and our man is standing on the dock waving as his ship sails out of sight. Tragedy, yes; demoralizing, yes again. As gays, we now have a choice. We may all climb back into our closets and wait out the storm which surely must come, or we can stand taller, act prouder and demand as gays our rights in a free society.

Personally, I have no intention of rebuilding my closet. I shall continue to live my life as a man and maintain those principles which make me unique against any opposition I may encounter from old "Tricky Dicky's Camp" (of fools), and I hope my brothers and sisters will join me in this goal. For even more than we are gay, we are free and it is just about time those "straight" perverts realize we are free.

Personally, if I am to be damned, then that judgment will come from my heavenly Father. And no man, woman or child shall judge me damned before that day.

Love,
Jack
Bay City, Michigan

Dear Jack,
Your spirit is the real spirit of an America we love.

170

•

FROM BEHIND BARS

When we edited a gay newspaper we often ran pen-pal ads for prisoners. We received the following letter from a prisoner who was delighted by the response to his ad from the gay community.

Dear Lige and Jack,
Beautiful, beautiful; that's all I can say to you wonderful people.

Thanks to you I've received nice letters from all over the country and it really made a change in my life. Even though I'm behind bars, it's so much better knowing people of your own kind and relating to them.

There have been individuals from all walks of life. Both young and old, passive and aggressive, gentle and those a bit strong. But, I love every last one of them and if I have to stay up till two a.m. every night answering them and trying to develop a friendship . . . I will!

To be truthful, I never felt there were that many wonderful people out there. I want to take this opportunity to express my sincere thanks for you giving of yourself in helping me through the night.

> Much warmth,
> Johnny R.
> Columbus, Ohio

Dear Johnny,
There are many lonely people who are not in prison who should stop their damned whining about being lonely and write to you

guys. Robert Ingersoll said: "The time to be happy is now. The place to be happy is here. The way to be happy is to make others so."

●

BILLY GRAHAM'S
GAY ADMIRER

Dear Sirs,
Your unwarranted attack on Billy Graham puts you in the "old queenie" class of reporting. Really, have you any reason for flogging this man who is really a much needed voice? Listen to him; you might find some value in what he has to say. He's not for all of us. Neither are you. So let him do his own thing —you're doing yours, eh? Tolerance is what you're preaching. Practice it.

Also, I resent your attack on the "hard hats." They are wonderful to the homosexual world. What trade! I find them loving, pleasant and most passionate. Maybe you met a disgruntled old meanie. Most of them I find very cooperative; and they had to do their thing. I'm for them! God bless America and the brave hard hats!

Charles W.
New York City

Dear Charles,
Billy Graham, who was a close friend of Richard Nixon, the patron saint of hard hats, attacked homosexuals in *Reader's Digest* (an appropriate spot) before we ventured to expose him.

Let's hope that one of those big brave hard hats (who'll let you grovel on your knees and blow him for trade) doesn't smash your Fundamentalist skull someday.

172

LOOKING FOR AN
IMPERSONATOR

Dear Lige and Jack,

Basically, my sexual inclinations are straight. I am pleased by females. However, I am aware that the human body is very complex and what may exist physically is not always that which exists mentally, emotionally. I am highly attracted to a person feminine by nature regardless of physical sex. I'm highly attracted to the female impersonator, the sincere cross-dresser.

Dayton, Ohio, is a very conservative town; therefore, there still remain on the books very stiff laws concerning dressing. As a result it is very hard to come into contact with the sincere female impersonator.

Could you suggest a couple of places where one might try to see a female-impersonator show, or that drag queens might frequent with ease?

> With Peace,
> Donald F.
> Dayton, Ohio

Dear Donald,

Most male cross-dressers are themselves "straight"—that is, they are attracted to women to such an extent that they wish to dress as women themselves. They seek admiration, but not sex from men. Only the gay transvestite is likely to enjoy a male's ministrations. Gay transvestites are fewer in number.

Check in the gay bars in nearby cities and ask where the cross-dressers go.

A MAN OF THE WORLD

Dear Lige and Jack,

I am what one might imagine to be the stereotyped heroic male. I am 38 years of age, 5'11'', 175 pounds and considered very handsome by my associates. I have lived the life of a soldier of fortune, having traveled every continent except Antarctica. I am a cum laude graduate, former college athlete and an active sportsman. I have had affairs with women of every race, creed and color during my adventurous career. One might imagine that I would be satisfied with this role. This is not so.

I have tried to suppress my homosexual desires because of the social taboos, fear of venereal disease and the fact that such a relationship is completely foreign to the life I have led. However, when I dwell on the issue a strange sensual lust and anticipation surges through my body. It has reached the point that I must find out once and for all if this is what I want. Is this strange? Is such a desire unusual? Am I really a homosexual? Or are all these desires natural and any suppression of them the result of centuries of ignorance and anticipated socio-religious customs?

I would appreciate any comments that will, I hope, help me to resolve the situation.

> Yours sincerely,
> "Bimbo"
> Portsmouth, N.H.

Dear Bimbo,

You're adventuresome. You say you must "find out once and for all." Find out more than once. Try it several times! One last request, however (and we don't mean to sound like overprotective mothers): please find the right man. Just *anybody* probably won't do, you know.

174

• • •

HURDLES

When the psychiatric establishment labels a gay person's feelings "pathological," and the religious establishment insists that they are "sinful," while the State calls for criminal sanctions against their expression, that person must, to say the least, take stock of himself.

He must ask himself if it isn't true that he's capable of being just as good and thoughtful as anybody else. If so, what is so "pathological" about his feelings? Whom do they injure, and how? A psychiatrist may say that they injure *him*. Again, how? If he examines such questions carefully he soon realizes that only the condemnation encouraged by the psychiatric establishment injures him, and this happens if he's taken in by unverified theories and persuaded he should feel tainted.

He must ask himself if the religious establishment has always been on target about other sexual questions. Birth control, for example? Or divorce? What about abortion? Premarital sex? Isn't it true that many clergymen once fought the introduction of anesthetics into maternity wards because they believed that Eve's "sin" had condemned all women to suffer pain in childbirth? Can any sensible person take such quackery seriously?

The State, naturally, bases its accusations of criminality on psychiatric and religious theories. Six states have already eliminated anti-homosexual statutes which prohibit relations between consenting adults. Other states, hopefully, will soon be equally as progressive.

175

In the meantime, the homosexually inclined person would do well to be equally skeptical of all these institutions which have condemned him. They've been wrong before, certainly, and it's quite plain to all but the most insistent conformists that they're making severe blunders today as well.

POPPERS

Gentlemen:

I have a few comments to make about poppers (amyl nitrate) and their effect.

Most of the consequences of a bad reaction are the same as those of a faint, that is, the result of decreased blood flow to vital organs, particularly the brain. The most effective way to deal with this is to place the subject in a horizontal position, and then slowly raise both his legs vertically. This returns blood to the heart and thus the rest of the circulation. This is the most important first-aid measure.

The amount of oxygen in the blood can be decreased by poppers. For most people this presents no danger because of the short period of time that it is in effect. But for blacks with sickle-cell disease there is the danger that a sickle-cell crisis could be brought about this way. I know of no instances where this has occurred, but see no reason why it could not. The possibility is real.

176

Certainly the best background to the use of any pharmacological agents is knowledge of what they can do (and this is not to advocate abuse).

Sincerely,
Lewis R., M.D.
New York, New York

Dear Doctor,
Thanks for sending us information about poppers.

We're down on them. Why? Poppers, it seems, are a head/body trip that we use to put between ourselves and another person. Direct contact without such an intermediary puts two people in tune on more realistic levels. Also, poppers make you tired, and have been known to wipe out more than a few exciting sexual episodes right in the middle.

•

A MOTHER'S PRIDE

Dear Lige and Jack,
I attended the Gay Pride March in New York this June. I'm no longer young, so I made it only from Sheridan Square to Forty-second Street. But I wanted to tell you how truly good it all was. The spirit, the friendliness, the courage and the joy was something I shall not ever forget. How I wished all my friends would have joined me.

Yes, I'm straight. I had pondered whether I would take along a sign urging "straights join in, support your brothers and sisters, your sons and daughters." Perhaps next time I will. This time I sort of felt I'd like to "walk with," not "for."

My son in San Francisco had told me to speak to older gay

177

people, that the younger ones would not want to be so friendly. But it did not work out that way. I was mixing in the crowd feeling a little shy and sort of "alone," when two young men saw my "PEACE" button and spoke to me themselves. We chatted easily. I said I was marching for my gay son in San Francisco and believe it or not, for an ex-daughter-in-law in San Francisco who came all the way to New York last year to tell me she had found love for the first time in her life, a woman. No wonder her life had been so troubled before. So we visited. They were gentle and beautiful. A few others heard us talking and they did me the honor of asking if I would like to walk with them.

All around me I saw happy faces. All the way along there were also cries of support. It was terribly hot and as I say I am not so young. Twelve grandchildren and one great-grand-son—but I forgot the heat and the fatigue as I took my place in the walk for freedom, for honesty and against bigotry. It was all beautiful and I still feel the warmth of the kindness around me.

> Sincerely,
> Sarah M.
> New York City

Dear Sarah,
Your letter is an inspiration, as, we're sure, you are to those around you. Were there more thoughtful parents like yourself it would make life easier for many people. How proud your son must be of you!

•

NOT A COMPLETE SOPHOMORE

Dear Lige and Jack,
Although I am not a homosexual I am not a complete sopho-

more in this area. I am close to several fellows who are homosexual to varying degrees. Also, I believe my studies in animal behavior at Cornell have given me some insight.

So, for what it's worth, I believe that homosexuals confuse strong affection with pure animal sexuality.

It is my belief, although I have not done any real research as yet, that homosexuals only *think* that they are experiencing greater pleasure, just as some heterosexual women think that they can attain true sexual pleasure with only their "true love" or whatever, and consequently do. Hence my advice—be an animal—don't think about it. Variety is the spice of life.

> Tom P.
> Cornell University

Dear Tom
We're not sure what you're talking about.

"Homosexuals" as a group aren't of any particular mind, which is a good reason to use this heavy word as an adjective (i.e., homosexually inclined person) instead of as a noun. Some confuse affection with sex, some infuse affection into sex, and the rest probably feel affectionate, hoping that sex will be one great expression, among many, of such feelings.

Some may think that their sex lives are more pleasurable, while others only wish that they might be as lucky in this respect as their neighbors, gay or straight.

As for you, dear student, you are just beginning your explorations. If you are not yet a "complete sophomore," your "variety" philosophy may someday make you a graduate student.

● ● ●

179

THE BIG MISTAKE

Newcomers to the gay social whirl are often guilty of a dreadful mistake. They make social judgments about the gay communities they observe without first asking questions about the total social environment.

If they see gays who are secretive, deceitful or self-deprecating, they may foolishly blame their traits on the fact that they're gay, failing to realize that society has brought about their behavior.

A kind of affection that's despised, scorned and ridiculed can't demonstrate, with ease, its *joie de vivre*.

WHAT ABOUT THE LAW?

Dear Sirs,

I often hear gay bars and prostitute houses are raided by officers. I am puzzled on laws. Baths are not new and I know some baths have been in business for several decades. I cannot find information on laws or baths in adult bookshops. I do not want to ask managers of the baths and clubs questions for my own protection. Are sexual acts in baths and clubs legal?

> Yours truly,
> Homer S.
> Hyattsville, Maryland

Dear Homer,

In most states, unfortuntely, sexual acts involving the mouth or the anal tract (between the same or opposite sexes) are illegal—whether in a bathhouse, a brothel, or in your own cozy bed.

But there are other laws which make this country great. One says that bed-bugging—that is, spying on fornicators—behind the doors of their private (rented) rooms is also illegal. So, as long as you aren't twiddling your diddler in public, no one should be able to arrest you unless, of course, you have invited witnesses to your bedside who will testify in court about the intricacies of your sodomistic predilections.

Some police districts send entrapment officers into gay locales to play knees in exchange for blow jobs. Upon completion of these blow jobs, they have been known to arrest the most talented lips among us. This unsavory practice is dying out, however, except in those areas where policemen prefer getting blow jobs to fighting real crime.

•

A SENIOR CITIZEN

Dear L & J,

In 1930 circumstances were such that I moved to another city. I was in my early twenties and there, away from the confines of home and family, I lived my gay life to the full. I was attractive, well off financially, had a lovely apartment and was able to satisfy my needs.

Then in the Forties I inherited a family, two young children. Their father was my late brother, their mother a nogoodnick who walked out on them. I was determined to bring these kids up properly, which meant abandoning the gay life and my friends. In fact we moved back here so I could start my life anew, in the role of parent. We came back in 1950 and since then I've had one "party" and no gay contacts.

The children are grown now. The girl is married, but the boy changed at adolescence and has been a constant source of worry ever since. I was drained of my financial resources paying for psychiatric help for the boy and for myself.

The one "party" I had occurred one night when I was feeling particularly depressed. He seemed most presentable. It was a pickup and foolishly I took him home. I was rolled and lost a cherished ring (a family heirloom), and was threatened with a knife at the throat. This experience shattered me. I guess even at my age I was "green" due to lack of experience.

The other day I filled out my senior citizen's pass for one-half fare on the subways and buses and that night I read an article by you. I realize my time is getting short. I yearn with a desperate longing for a few more "parties" before my time is up, but I'm so scared.

Is there a brothel that's safe? I've very little to recommend me. I'm sixty-five but personable. I'm intelligent and kind.

I've let my hair down and I feel better. This is the first "dish" I've had in over twenty years, so please excuse me if my gay lingo is dated.

I must still remain discreet, yet I had to get this off my chest. Some days are worse than others; I can hardly stand this repression any further, thus my need to write to you.

> Michael S.
> Detroit, Michigan

Dear Michael,
Your local gay organization should be able to steer you to a place in your town where you may safely meet men of like tastes.

182

Your letter from "the closet" touched us deeply. You've lived for others and have given your love to them in your own way. Walt Whitman sings to you, dear friend, in a poem called "To You." He says:

I will leave all and come and make hymns of you . . .
Oh I could sing such grandeurs and glories about you.
You have not known what you are,
You have slumbered upon yourself all your life . . .
There is no endowment in man or woman that is not tallied in
   you.
There is no virtue, no beauty in man or woman, but as good is
   in you,
No pleasure waiting for others, but an equal pleasure waits
   for you.

●

A GEORGIA PEACH

Dear L & J,
I'm twenty-years-old and have tried hard to find a guy that would love and care for me. But in a way I'm afraid. When I was seventeen, I gave myself to another guy. I gave him the brush-off because most of my friends in my hometown knew he was a homosexual. To protect myself I began going steady with a girl whom I'm still dating. This girl says she loves me, but I don't love her. When I take her out, I just look at other guys and wonder what they would be like to make love with. I'm now living away from home and away from the family pressure, but I just don't know how to pick up or be friendly with other guys. I'm about to go out of my mind from loneliness here in Atlanta. Can you recommend a way to meet other guys like myself?

Anyone who has found happiness in this type of existence is lucky, for I have not found any as of yet.

L.J.
Atlanta, Georgia

Dear Lonely,
How do you expect to find happiness when you're paralyzed by fear? Your fears have created a deceitful situation in which you toy with your girl friend's emotions for no other reason than to hide your own. Think of other people for a change. Get out and explore the world.

Life in Atlanta swings. There are lots of bars, baths, parties and dances. If you can stop being fearful, you'll be much happier. At least you've recognized your fear, which puts you many steps ahead of those who haven't. Your battle is half won. Remember: this is a new age! To be different is not to be indecent. If the occasion arises, stand up for your right to live and love as you see fit and be an individual. Happiness isn't the result of luck. Be open to yourself and to others. If your girl friend is only a cover-up be fair and stop fooling her.

• • •

IT IS NOT WHAT OTHERS DO

A happy life is, in great part, a product of character. Character is fate. Ideally it might include a care for one's own health and a devotion to honesty, gaiety, self-reliance, and curiosity. The ability to defy convention rests somewhere near its center.

Happiness should not depend on what others think of us, but on what we think of ourselves. "It is not what others

184

do or do not do that is my concern," said Buddha, "but what I do and what I do not do, *that* is my concern." To bolster self-approval becomes our task.

Popular songs are filled with such lyrics as "I'm no good without you," or "I can't live without you." People wander through life believing that only the company of a lover makes them whole. This is the worst sort of nonsense. Getting a lover is not the ultimate panacea. Relying on another to provide us with a sense of self is the deadliest of poisons not only for relationships that are underway but for those we hope to begin. A person who feels this way is easy to spot. Others sense that he is seeking a serenity from lovers that he doesn't enjoy himself. This means that he has a diminished inner core—that he falls short of being a person in his own right—and he seems less interesting and attractive as a result.

FROM A YOUNG MAN

Dear Lige and Jack,
I am eighteen and gay and I have put several weeks of thought into this letter wishing to sound neither maudlin, self-serving, nor self-pitying. The rhetoric of this letter may sound odd to you in that I am a homosexual with an urban consciousness captive in a rural environment.

185

Now before the quick-witted urbanites yell, "What cause does he have to complain, we're all oppressed!" I'd like to write about what it's been like to be gay and live in rural Kentucky.

Merle Miller had it right when he said, "I started packing to leave Marshalltown when I was two." Though admittedly an exaggeration it seemingly captures the mood of rural homosexuals, or rather mine at least. I can't truthfully speak for other rural homosexuals, having never knowingly met one. I don't know, I maybe brushed alongside one on the sidewalk, maybe looked one in the eyes, maybe actually met one and talked to one, but as I said, never knowingly. You see, *no one* here admits to sexual unorthodoxy. If one did one would well be burned at the stake for sexual heresy.

This part of the country and its people are somewhat unique and may someday become famous in that it will undoubtedly be the last stronghold of the Archie Bunkers of this country. Assuming, as Merle Miller did of McCarthyism, that Bunkerism will ever subside.

There aren't any Jews here so people don't get a chance to call them "kike." But perhaps that's because they wouldn't know what that meant. There are blacks, though, and to the people they're "niggers." Women's liberation is a joke—to the women. Homosexuals? Well, a friend of Merle Miller said as related in his book, "Straights don't want to know for sure, and they can never forgive you for telling them. They prefer to think it doesn't exist, but if it does, at least keep quiet about it." As far as I can tell, and I have lived in one county for eighteen years, everyone here is straight. Homosexuality? All is quiet on the central front. It is possible that I was the only person in the county voting for George McGovern.

I have read extensively on the subject of homosexuality and a brief bibliography would include Dr. Eustace Chesser's *Strange Loves* from England, the brilliantly conceived and

186

superbly executed *Sexual Politics* by Kate Millett, the exhausting yet informative Arno Karlen's *Sexuality and Homosexuality*, two issues of liberating GAY, and my favorite, Merle Miller's *On Being Different: What It Means To Be A Homosexual*. I am looking forward to reading E.M. Forster's *Maurice,* your own book, *I Have More Fun With You Than Anybody,* and Peter Fisher's *The Gay Mystique: The Myth and Reality of Male Homosexuality*. Sorry if I've bored you with my reading habits, but rural homosexuals must be reassured that somewhere there are people like themselves.

On Being Different remains my favorite for reasons which are obvious. First, its author speaks eloquently and courageously for us and for himself, and secondly, because his and my small town childhood were so very much the same.

It is superfluous for me to say I have suffered from the loneliness and despair of being a sexual pariah among the smug and bigoted straight world, for haven't we all? However, I can say with a strong and honest conviction that there is not an inkling of gay life in the rural community. I will, however, admit that my ostracism was to a certain degree self-inflicted.

There is a tradition of strong anti-intellectualism here and since I was a little precocious for my age I was obviously a "sissy" and a "queer." I was quite frequently singled out with such epithets but of course never by the words "faggot," "pansy," "fruitcake," or "fairy." Very few here have a repertoire of homosexual put-down words which extend beyond the proverbial "sissy" or "queer." I had no idea what "queer" meant when I began school but as I got older I realized it meant that I was different. Different in the most despicable way. And somehow I knew it was true, after all. Nobody at school had had sex with their older brothers since the age of five. And I continued to have till I was thirteen; my brother being seventeen at that point became interested in girls.

Our family was associated with a quite unpopular minority

187

religion and that also alienated me from my friends and increased my awareness that I was different; sissy, queer, odd. Besides, when it came to homosexuality they pronounced with all the vigor of their self-righteous piety, ''Men who lie with other men shall not inherit the kingdom of God.'' I am now uncertain about the existence of that God.

We have always been poor but so are a lot of other people around here so that didn't really bother me except that the rich, whom I so hated and so envied, were always supercilious and condescending. What really bothered me was what my mother would say, ''Your brother was supposed to have been a girl and you really weren't supposed to be here.'' I doubt that Iowans have a monopoly on that little maternal tidbit but it would seem so since my mother is also from Iowa. I didn't lapse into any trauma over her words but I knew I had been an accident.

My loneliness through high school was bearable but growing worse. Then college offered some hope. Social Security would pay tuition, and I was sure to find some gay people there. I went to a state college about sixty miles from home (too close) and majored in English and journalism. I liked it reasonably well and did well, but I began to realize I was in for another disappointment—no gay life. Besides, I wasn't ready to come out of the closet and I lacked the courage to do little more than stare at the graffiti on the walls of the men's room and wonder if what was scrawled there was a lonely and desperate cry or merely a prank by heterosexuals to get a laugh when the telephone number was called.

I live at home with my mother which makes my involvement in the gay world very risky. She doesn't know I'm homosexual but she has a suspicion since I read so much about it. We have talked a lot about homosexuality and I know enough that I can never reveal to her what I am.

I've wanted to move from Kentucky for some time and since last fall I've had my hopes set on New York City. However,

188

finances have kept me from it and is and will keep me from it. As of now, I have been unsuccessful in finding a job. The best one can hope for around here is $1.60 an hour.

I'll be nineteen next month and my lottery number is thirty-four. I'd like to tell the Army I'm a homosexual but not here. Not in this state. The result would be scandalous and I do not want my family to suffer because of my sexuality. Don't get me wrong, more than anything else I want to come out of the closet. I want to become involved in the movement in the gayest sense of the word. But first I must move to where the movement is. I have to leave this part of the country before long, I have to join the movement, I have to come out of the closet. Perhaps I'll come back when family situations are different and call other gays out, but first I *must* leave. How I don't know because that takes money and right now this all looks like a hopeless dream.

But now I've done what I hoped I wouldn't—sound self-pitying. So cheers, I'm coming out. I'll get there somehow but I'll be there to give a hopeful credence to "Gay is Good," "Gay is Proud." And also to Forster's words: "I believe in aristocracy . . . Not an aristocracy of power, based upon rank and influence, but an aristocracy of the sensitive, the considerate, and the plucky. Its members are to be found in all nations and classes, and through all the ages, and there is a secret understanding between them when they meet. They represent the true human tradition, the one queer victory of our race over cruelty and chaos."

> Love and peace to you all.
> Your gay friend,
> Curtis B.
> Kentucky

Dear Curtis,
If a young man who lives in a rural community can learn as

189

much as you have without meeting even one other homosexually inclined person, liberation is penetrating remote territories. There are other bright, isolated people who are members of the "aristocracy of the sensitive, the considerate and the plucky" just as you are. Before long, no doubt, you'll start meeting them.

● ● ●

GAY LIBERATION

Our approach to gay liberation is primarily a personal one. This is not to say that we haven't done our share of political maneuvering. We've agitated from both outside and inside the system. Such agitation is still necessary, although gay lib must now be quick to adopt new techniques and strategies to be effective. Street demonstrations and "zaps" aren't as consequential today as they once were.

Gay liberation, like all popular mass movements, goes through cycles and stages. Sometimes it surfaces proudly, as it did in the years following the Stonewall riots in Greenwich Village in 1969. Then, the number of active groups in the country jumped from approximately forty to over four hundred.

At other times the movement is somewhat dormant and its work proceeds quietly in the courts as courageous individuals in various professions, teachers, doctors, librarians, scientists, lawyers, government employees, step forward to contest the restrictions that society has placed on them. It goes forward, somewhat unnoticed too, in the consciousness of a national gay community that is rapidly becoming aware of the fact that homosexual inclinations are, as Dr. Franklin E. Kameny has put it, "not only not

190

immoral, but moral, in a real and positive sense and good and right and desirable both for the individual and for society."

Independent gay liberation organizations, scattered throughout the nation, are as capable, trustworthy and knowledgeable as the people at their helms. What happens in all movements has happened, in certain locales, to gay lib too, and that is that bright ideas fall out of the hands of innovators and pioneers into the laps of do-gooders, bureaucrats, academics and administrative plodders. The most effective gay lib spokesmen and leaders are those who, along with a strong sense of what it means to be a civil libertarian and an activist protector of one's community, also have a personal touch and take time to laugh. We trust people like these. Generally gay lib groups are often fine places for men and women to go if they've little or no knowledge of the gay subculture and its ways. Those who are "coming out" can usually count on first-rate treatment from activists. If there were no other reason this alone would justify the existence of gay lib organizations.

The noisy political rah rah "2-4-6-8 Gay is just as Good as Straight," (or) "3-5-7-9 Lesbians are Mighty Fine" slogans may sound a bit corny today, though when they were first introduced as thousands of women and men marched in gay parades through the streets of American and Canadian cities, they had a certain flair.

Gay liberation for many young men and women, is an intensely viable and important experience. For others, who've passed through its portals, it is a fondly remembered stage in their lives, one which helped them come to terms with themselves.

Aside from political advances, assaults on U.S. government policies, the turnabouts of some churches and the rising consciousness of the homosexually inclined masses, the areas of greatest growth of gay liberation recently, have been in the universities, colleges and in neighborhoods.

University lib groups reach young people at crucial stages in their development, providing them with information that hoists self-confidence and promotes a sane perspective. These groups also reach their surrounding communities, sending speakers to clubs, churches and academic groups. In many colleges, gay liberation is funded, as are other university organizations, by annual contributions approved by the student councils.

Neighborhood groups, contrasting in their approach with the inner-city activists, are springing up everywhere too, providing socials, discussions and dances. In our own neighborhood a community center has opened its doors and a group of well-intentioned people gather almost every evening to talk to one another honestly, to improve their mutual understanding, to relax, read, play chess, take art classes, participate in drama groups, and to gain a greater sense of self-awareness and concern for the quality of life itself, realizing that their attitudes about sensuality and sexuality and their life-styles contribute to the enhancement of their lives and that of those close to them.

There are now enough first-rate books which have emerged from gay liberation to serve as a basis for discussions. The movement is moving into living rooms where, at regular weekly socials, friends discuss their hopes, dreams, problems and philosophies openly. They give their best thoughts to friends and receive the same in return. Gay liberation is finding its grass roots, stepping out of meeting halls into people's closest relationships: those with their neighbors and friends.

While excellent work (political and social) is being done by many gay organizations, newspapers and magazines, gay liberation is much more than a movement, in any political sense. It does not depend on any one person, on any single publication, or on any special group. It is a *feeling*, or an *attitude*. It's a personal attitude toward oneself and toward life that's affirmative. Gay liberation can be the soul property of *anybody*, no matter what his or her sexual orientation. At its basis, we think, is what Whitman called "the institution of the dear love of comrades," something much wider and much more expansive than what is imagined by those who'd confine it to exclusively homosexual interests.

We would like to see gay liberation moving in directions that view sexuality as multi-dimensional, closer to the old hippie slogan, "If it moves fondle it." Whitman characterized himself as "the caresser of life, wherever moving."

To categorize, label, pigeonhole and catch ourselves in only one form of sexual expression, makes us static, one-dimensional. Homosexual inclinations are the birthright of every man and not the distinct, isolated desire pattern of a few, of a minority, that is. We view sexuality, in contrast to exclusive homosexual or heterosexual distinction, as an adventure that jumps boundaries and is wide-flowing, intensely curious and almost lushly undifferentiated in its pursuit of beings to love. Homosexual feelings are a potential joy latent, waiting to be discovered, in all people on various levels. They are a natural, or in fact, a principal human propensity in everyman/woman. This perspective bypasses genitals and goes into the most fundamental depths of the touch, the caress and an unstructured feeling and appreciation for all living things and their pulsating variety.

We have seen for ourselves proof positive that gay liberation is having an astoundingly healthy effect on young lives. When we addressed the Plenary Session of the 26th Annual Conference on World Affairs at the University of Colorado (Boulder) on March 16, 1973, we were surrounded by a gay community (college-aged women and men) who seemed to us the very cream of American civilization. They were extraordinarily relaxed, honest, buoyant and full of good humor. These young people shared an appreciation for themselves and for their community that was well justified. They seemed proud of themselves and of the idyllic spot in which they lived. When people *feel* beautiful, they act beautifully. Their states of mind become apparent in their way of being present.

These kids took us into the great national parks. They lent us boots so we could climb with them through the woods and trudge through the snow. We shed our New York clothes and donned their Colorado duds. They pointed out to us those incredible spaces that still give America an awesome beauty and where miracles are commonplace, opening expansive vistas to us that we'd never seen before. Giant peaks. Snowcapped majesties. "When I stopped going daily into the mountains for at least an hour," said one of our youthful hosts, "I realized what a dreadful mistake I was making and got back into the right habit again."

What did these truly gay young men and women teach us? That there are delightful places in this sometimes confusing world where extraordinary developments are taking place in minds and spirits. That the future is certainly filled with bright things. That the present is only dark if our present perspective makes it so.

There are many places where life sings. For us—on that occasion—it was Colorado. For others it may be some other pulsating locale. But wherever it is, it tells us more often than we sometimes admit that the sweetest vibrations and the best intentions are moving forward and are rapidly becoming realities.